# return not desired

by taylor church

# acknowledgments

Some writers thrive in solitude and reclusiveness. If it was up to them, editors, critics, and publishers wouldn't exist. In their utopian ideal people would just line up to read their masterpieces that were created in quite damp rooms and luxurious lofts, and would receive them for the works of genius they truly were. Not a word would be changed, and not a a single suggestion would be given. Although that does sound kind of nice sometimes, I am not of that fold. I need people. I need input. I need people to tell me my sentences don't makes sense, and I need people to stroke my ego by telling me my metaphors are beautiful and ethereal. Thus, in my own process, a multitude of thanks is required.

A special thanks to my parents who understand my dream and would cheer me on tirelessly if I had only sold one book. Thanks to Brittany who read my manuscript on a hospital bed. Thanks to Dani for her artistic eye and sisterly love. Thanks to Lydia Ripplinger for her vast knowledge of the English language. Thanks to Nick Jorgensen who helped in more ways than he knows. Thanks to Katie Christensen for reading a very early draft that should have been read by no one. Thanks to Drew Tadd for his photography and friendship. Thanks to

Sila Koç for her keen eye that helped create a most pleasing cover. Thanks to Gavin Anderson for his last minute help and expertise. Thanks to William Lam for his motivational texts at 2:00 a.m.

An oversensitive thanks to those who have read my work and encouraged me to write more. People rarely realize when a kind, timely word can change a life.

For Brittany, as she made this journey happen

# preface

When people ask me "So what's this next book about?," it tends to coil my insides just a little bit. I want to respond with some pedantic and perfectly timed riposte about how any good book is about more than one specific thing, or how art cannot be labeled before it is even finished. But you've got to give people something. The truth is, this book is a genre hybrid: part motivational, part historical, part memoir, and part incoherent pseudo-philosophy babble.

I was never certain where I wanted the book to go, but I knew what I was getting down on paper was important even if it was only intelligible to my own brain. The trouble with writing is while you are immersed in a project it's hard to tell if it's catnip or a masterpiece. And I wrestled with this problem through various notebooks, cold nights typing in my kitchen, and months without writing a single word.

In case you have read my first book and were hoping for a sequel, this is not it. I assume the title and cover will give that away. But I want to cover my bases. I would hate for someone to be thirty pages in, reading about a death camp, wondering when the romance chapters are going to come. They are not. Thanks for your interest in my first book, but this is nothing of that type. Maybe a sequel will come, but for now I have rerouted to a different genre.

Lastly, this book is not to inform the uninformed about the Holocaust, nor is it an academic piece for the serious scholar; it's a book about life. So if you have life, this book is for you.

*There was a hunger for more tales of simultaneous horror and deliverance. I did not pause to ask what that said of my nature. Writers don't.*

~Thomas Keneally

# chapter 1

*"All that we see or seem is but a dream within a dream."*

~Edgar Allen Poe

I got dropped off at the bus stop later than usual today. Basketball practice went long. I'm exhausted and just happy to return home to something familiar. It's hot outside. It's usually toasty in Phoenix, but this heat is anomalous for January.

As my feet nonchalantly caress the sidewalk in the same pattern they have followed countless times, something thrusts my eyes upward from my normal feet-watching gaze. I notice a dusty cloud enveloping my neighborhood. I don't panic, for I'm used to intense monsoon storms. But the dust persists and climbs all around me. My feet move quicker until a nervous jog ensues.

I am only two blocks from home, but suddenly I am lost. I recognize that I am not far, but somehow I've taken a weird turn, placing me in an unknown graffiti-ridden alley. Just above the cinderblock fences and large black trash cans, I see myriad spikes, made of metal and wood. I see remnants of broken glass and torn machines in the distance. I am still perplexed beyond comprehension. The images seem to multiply before my very eyes. I still have a vague idea of the proximity of my house, but it now appears less and less likely that I will return anytime soon. I can feel dirt on my teeth.

The brown dust intensifies, obstructing my vision and adding to my weighted confusion. The ominous surroundings leave me momentarily paralyzed. Is some sinister and far off force attempting to destroy me? Is this the end? I'm not ready. I'm too young. But the clouds of pulverized dirt encircle me, as do the never before seen objects of terror. I start to choke as my lungs fill up with gusts of thick dust, but I know I must fight. I must leave this labyrinth. If I can just reach my cul-de-sac, I'll be fine. But I'm not fine. The houses around me are missing parts. Roofs are tattered, pools are emptied, and doors are smashed and covered with thick black marks and terrible dents. Usually I run into people on my way home. Maybe Jeff; certainly Ashley. Not now. I'm utterly and terrifyingly alone. Doom approaches and I wish for anything else but this. The end is imminent, but I don't know by what force. If I weren't full of anxious adrenaline, I would be crying. In the distance I see rubble and smashed machinery of all kinds. My head pounds and I prepare for a swift finishing of life, an erasing of all I've ever known. My muscles clench and my eyes shut like a castle door. My youth is about to be deleted.

# chapter 2

> *"Serious moral inquiry cuts close to the bone of the investigator."*
>
> ~Daniel Jonah Goldhagen

I wake up. It's 3:21 a.m. I'm twenty-seven years old. I haven't been on a school bus for years, and I have long since left the sun and concrete of urban Arizona. I'm alone in a cheap hotel room in Warsaw, Poland. A familiar song reverberates in my foggy head. Its chorus repeats the simplistic and symbolic words, "I'm coming home, I'm coming home." I go to the bathroom and return to bed wondering what elicited such a vivid and frightful dream.

When I wake up several hours later, the morning fog in my head has dissipated. It becomes clear that the great vividness of my dream was not without reason, I'm just not positive what that reason is yet. I was in Poland for the express purpose of seeing the Auschwitz Concentration Camp in the southern corner of the country. Maybe the horror, the darkness of it all was made manifest in my dream to prepare me, as a sort of loose parable.

Ever since I learned what the Holocaust was, I've been obsessed. But how can somebody be so enthralled with such a macabre chapter of history? Is it some sinister element that has genetically made its way into my blood? It is doubtful. Human beings are drawn to things that make their hearts pulsate uncontrollably. This is why we listen to sad songs and watch depressing films even when we are not especially downtrodden. It's not that we have a dark and enigmatic side or a melancholy soul. Just the opposite, in fact. We are those who look at the polarity of human emotion and are moved. Perhaps we are moved to tears, or self-reflection, or better yet, in extreme cases of greatness, we are moved to action.

Herein is where we find a glorious paradox. Through studying tragedy and examining malicious behavior, we can actually become better people, but not in the "how-to" sense. Obviously we know we shouldn't kill, we shouldn't mistreat people, and we should act decently towards one another. The lessons to be gleaned here are deeper. And for a while now, or rather as long as I can remember, I was cognizant of this fact. I didn't understand it fully when I was younger, as it is with most things of true importance. I understood the concept more and more as I turned the pages of *The Diary of Anne Frank*, and as I read the timeless words of Elie Wiesel. And now, years later, with a foot and a shoulder in the doorway of adulthood, I still don't understand it fully. And I know I never will. But it has become my quest, and unknowingly my duty to figure it out the best I can.

What follows is my feeble attempt, as a gentile, a foolish *shegetz*[1], to understand and benefit from the horrors of yesterday. I know I will fall short, but I know the journey, for me at least, is essential.

---

[1] A boy or man who is not Jewish.

A couple hours later I woke up, grabbed some bread and a curious piece of European ham, and boarded the bus. The sun was just gaining the courage to show itself over the horizon. The air was brisk but pleasant. We were en route to Auschwitz. I knew there was no way to fully prepare myself mentally for the experience I was about to have, but I tried. I sat in the back of the bus, near the window, and started reading a book about Holocaust survival called *I Shall Live*. The account I read of a poor Polish man being viciously corralled from one concentration camp to another somehow eased my mind as I wanted all other worldly thoughts flushed from my head. I knew it was unlikely that I would ever return to Poland, let alone be able to visit the Auschwitz camp again, so I wanted the experience to be life-changing, paradigm shifting. I wanted all trivialities and silly worries to be temporarily erased from my thoughts. I had to be clear and ready.

The trip from Warsaw to the town of Oświęcim took us nearly four hours by bus. I sat there imagining the stark and cruel difference between my "trip" to Auschwitz, and that of those who were imprisoned there some seventy years ago. I had muttered complaints of not having enough leg room on the bus. And also I was bugged that we weren't stopping for a full meal, just some snacks in a small town with lots of z's in its name and a windmill in sight. How spoiled and selfish could I be? I had been destroyed by modernity and first world amenities. And history, the wise old codger it was, kept reminding me of how ungrateful I was being with bursts of humbling whispers that stayed with me all 315 kilometers of the trip.

As I sat on my cool, cushioned seat, the images in my mind were of countless inmates, the victims of Hitler's hate, helpless people being packed into metal boxes designed for cattle transportation, entered my brain. I could hear the cries of children and smell the sweat and feces that permeated throughout their "journey." Our course was the same, yet it could not be more different. Though those images in my head were vivid and real, they were only there through the power of literature, the emotion of documentaries and films I had seen, and the passion of certain history professors I had learned from. I had no real way of picturing the horror that was a reality for millions. But I tried. I felt that the least I could do was to try and sympathize, even if it was at the lowest possible level.

I felt like a kid desperately trying to understand the emotions of a grieving parent. A little boy can never fully appreciate the love of his mother or the protective instincts of his father until he is a parent. He can sympathize and imagine, but what he thinks and what really is are two different realities. And thus it was with me. I wanted to connect with the martyrs of yesterday; I wanted to somehow understand their plight. And as I turned pages and closed my eyes, I tried, woefully aware of my shortcomings.

I started seeing street signs directing us closer and closer to the haunting town that had become a place of sadism, death, and unspeakable terror by the Nazi regime. What was once Oświęcim had become Auschwitz during the war, and now decades later it was once again the Polish Oświęcim.

I saw quaint houses on one side of the road, and rusty tracks on the other. As we entered the town I saw a complete lack of recreation. A morose feeling crept up into me and left me dark and chilled. But I knew this was just the beginning. Women worked in their gardens and children walked home from school. Graffiti littered the walls and men worked on repaving the streets. For some reason I had expected the town to be more barren, more abandoned and run down. Oświęcim wasn't thriving or booming; however, it was living, it was producing, and it was existing.

As the bus turned left I could see red brick and chimneys. I knew we had arrived. The camp was massive, but only a small portion was visible through the trees and adjacent buildings. I took out my headphones and prepared for the very moment I had dreamed about ever since I learned what the Germans had done in Auschwitz.

I had done my research and knew that there was a small museum area with bathrooms, money exchange centers, and a bookstore. It was designed to look like the rest of Auschwitz, austere and bricked. But it was not part of the original structure. I was sure that most people there didn't know that. In fact, I was confident that I knew more about this place than the vast majority of the annoying tourists that were there, sharing the day with me.

The bus parked right next to another bus on one side and some vans on the other. We barely had enough room to get out. The place was packed. Hundreds of students and adults alike milled about the entrance gabbing and adjusting their camera settings. Our tour guide informed us that our tour would not commence for forty-five minutes. This news thrilled me. I wanted to see everything, and this included the bathrooms (that were not free) and the makeshift bookstore. I wanted a little solitude before we entered the gates.

I went and exchanged my euros for zloty so I could purchase a book or two. After the cost of travel, I had virtually no money left over for souvenirs and trinkets, but I couldn't help myself. The bookstore was tiny, but filled with beautiful tomes that I wouldn't find anywhere else. The lovely and buxom attendant of Polish descent, tall with a dark blouse and wonky teeth, directed me to the English section. I asked her what her favorite book was in an affable attempt to make small talk.

She responded with a shotgun list of quintessential texts and personal favorites. She explained to me which titles were required reading in Polish secondary schools and what authors had made appearances and given speeches at Auschwitz. For a bibliophile and amateur historian it was a priceless experience. While we sat talking and exchanging an occasional laugh, dozens of Asians came in and out, purchasing a book or poster without the slightest semblance of dialogue. I settled on a recently published book called *But I Survived*. First released in Polish, this was the first edition in English and was appropriately published by the Auschwitz-Birkenau State Museum. I didn't even know they published books. But I knew I wouldn't find this text in any used book store in America, so I paid the sixty zloty[2] and exited.

    I took my book and followed a tiny trail through the grass to a tree and some shade against a fence that had likely been erected decades before I came into this world. I was only forty or fifty yards removed from my group, but I needed the distance. I cracked open my new book and read just one line. The dedication read, "To my murdered colleagues and all victims of the Holocaust." It was simple and painfully pithy. I put the book back into its bag and made sure the receipt was still accessible. I wanted an authentic documentation of my purchase. I

---

[2] About 15 U.S. dollars.

wanted a piece of paper from Poland that had the word Oświęcim stamped on it.

It was hot and I was wearing a black T-shirt and jeans. I rolled up my jeans to my shins and sat down in the European dirt. I only had a few minutes before our tour commenced, but I had to think. I had to pray. I closed my eyes and asked God for a moment of clarity. I asked for a sense of understanding and an appreciation of erstwhile suffering. I paused and gathered my thoughts, then asked my Heavenly Father for peace in my heart. I asked for love to fill my soul and for my experience to make me a better person. I knew seeing the gas chambers and walking through hallowed grounds could change me. But I had to make sure that it did. If not, what was it all for, some photographs and education? It had to be about more. Warmness filled my body, and I knew I was ready.

I looked towards the main entrance and saw white birds flying around in what looked like figure eights. I thought about how eternally free those birds were and how their whiteness and freedom contrasted so greatly with the victims of Auschwitz, the ghosts behind the barbed wire fences. Everything around me seemed to take on some frightening symbolic form. I saw a raucous group of young adults smoking and throwing their trash on the ground as if we were not near a holy place, as if we weren't face to face with a giant and disturbing mausoleum. I noticed what a clear and beautiful

June day it was. I sat there under that foreign tree of untold knowledge and wondered how many truly clear days the inmates would have had there, or if the smoke from the chimneys made azure skies an impossibility.

    I got up and milled about around the talkative and jovial. I couldn't be bothered to talk to anyone. I am usually of a gregarious disposition, but I was not that day. I wanted that day immortalized in my mind, and I could not let trite conversations get in the way of my search for existentialism.

# chapter 3

*"For the camps are in us all."*

~Konnilyn G. Feig

Finally, our German tour guide motioned for us to form a line and head towards the entrance. I was confusingly excited and scared. But what was I scared of? Tour guides and non-functioning electric fences? Was I scared some Nazi on a horse was going to come back from time and cast me out with the others? Maybe I was just afraid of the past, frightened it would become all too real, too present. Maybe I feared feeling nothing. Or perhaps I was scared my own demons would awake and mingle with the saints of Europe, two groups unready to meet. I barely understood my own imagination. But sometimes at midday your imagination can be just as jumbled and reckless as it is in your dreams.

We walked through the portion of the museum where we were counted and given headsets. Suddenly my wild brain raced backwards in time remembering how all who entered Auschwitz during WWII were counted and marked with permanent reminders of their incarceration, dark ink-laden reminders, if they somehow survived to remember. Others who were viciously gassed upon arrival were not so lucky to be among those who were counted, tattooed, and stamped with indelible punctures and pigments.

I wondered if some people going through the turnstile received an odd feeling of déjà vu, recollecting sweaty days at Disneyland, or uncomfortable bustling to enter a metro station. It felt a little bit like the carnival-ization of something sacred and serious. But I tried to remember the sharp words of Harper Lee: "As sure as time, history is repeating itself, and as sure as man is man, history is the last place he'll look for his lessons." I myself was having some paradoxical form of déjà vu, remembering an event I was never present for. But that is the power of history and the brain. Things from the past, things we have never seen or touched have the power to jump forward in time when they have been studied and well absorbed in our minds.

As I shuffled through the line, more thoughts surged into my mind. I wondered what the prisoners would have felt if someone had told them that "one day thousands, even millions of people would pay money to enter the gates of Auschwitz." And though the circumstances in the camp were drastically different, there I was, paying to enter.

*ARBEIT MACHT FREI* was the slogan atop the black Iron Gate that led into the main camp. These words, though in German, hit me hard, so sardonically cruel, so mendacious and false: "Work Sets You Free," what a colossal crock. Did the Nazis actually think frozen and emaciated prisoners that smelled burning human flesh and saw murderous acts of sadism everyday would look up at those words and believe them, and work harder for the Aryan[3] cause? They could not have been so obtuse. They knew what they were doing, and they did it with an evil smile. I noticed the *B* was upside-down. I knew that prisoners had made this particular sign. In fact it was believed that the misplaced letter was an act of defiance by the inmates. I smiled at this small and beautiful piece of poetic justice as I gazed upward.

Our tour guide was in her mid-thirties, was trim, and had a pleasant face. But she spoke fast. There was a lot of information to cover and an enormous complex of buildings and sites to see in but a few hours. We were instructed to put our headsets on and turn to channel eight so that we could hear our tour guide speak over the scattered noise and unfamiliar languages of other groups.

Before we had passed through the gate, at the entrance point to Auschwitz, I had fallen behind and joined a different group with a different radio channel. This new instructor was a little older, a little craggier, but spoke with the same accented rapidity as the first.

I started to feel a surge of anxiety, like I might miss something, like I was in a massive graveyard and might skip over an important gravestone. But my desire to know and to feel were

---

[3] In Nazi racial theory this word denoted those corresponding with the Nordic physical ideal of Nazi Germany, otherwise known as the master race.

greater than this anxious feeling that twisted in my stomach. Again, the group marched forward and I stayed back, wanting to experience things myself. I didn't want to feel like it was a field trip, though that's exactly what it was for some of the people there.

I looked all around me. To my right were two young men filming a documentary. Straight ahead was endless acreage of brick and barbed wire fences, to my left were more red buildings and chimneys in the distance. Behind me was the past, a completely separate non-suffering world, the outside.

I slowly inched forward, taking notice of every vestige of the past that I could. As crowded as it was, it was nothing compared to the melee of actual prisoners entering the camp. There was noise and smells for us, but they weren't odious; they weren't screaming and reeking of death.

I shuffled forward and saw the "kitchen" where the inmates were given inhuman portions of gruel, perhaps with a cup of coffee, and if they were lucky some rotten bread, all of which was likely to cause violent bouts of diarrhea and the often fatal dysentery. My stomach curled as we passed this building. We didn't even go inside, but I still shook my head in dismay at man's ability to torture. I wondered if I had tortured any person in any tiny way. My insides coiled at the very thought.

The ground was dusty and full of remnants of cobblestone and faded brickwork. We walked up to the first building we would enter and my heart froze as I thought of the past and felt a tinge of atavistic guilt. How could men, brothers, and fathers I could be distantly related to concoct such a network of killing machines and misanthropic ideas? I took a step back, falling further behind my group. I examined the steps, the windows and the block. Block 16. I entered the concrete building, constructed by the bloody hands of weary martyrs. It was ill lit and damp. Our group crowded and bustled along, listening to our tour guide's explanation of each room.

The rooms had been restored in various ways, but kept their unmistakable eeriness. Plaques and signs in several languages had been mounted and raised to remind tourists of the facts and the terrifying statistics of Nazi power. I wanted to stay in each room for an hour, taking pictures and reading every line of every monument and mosaic. But time only permitted a few minutes in each room. We were all in a reverent rush.

All of the barracks and various chambers blended together in a cacophonous blur. Every gray corridor, each alcove, and each antechamber revealed harsh truths, truths I already knew about, but that this time hit me with full force, with their entire weight.

Each block, be it Block 21, Block 6, or Block 13, had a purpose or educational theme. In a way we meandered through these buildings just like an art museum, observing traces of the past, and taking in knowledge at Mach speed. But it wasn't a happy museum with colorful Rembrandts and vivacious colors; it was a museum of the dead, with displays of dark reminders of unforgettable sins and untold suffering. I would never know the names of the little boys that clutched their mothers and cried at night. I would never know the games the little girls would play to distract themselves from the horror and death around them.

All the rooms touched me and carelessly tossed about my emotions, but one section of the camp took hold of my heart and squeezed it without the slightest modicum of mercy. This was the section of the camp where the seized items of the inmates were held. Upon arrival in the camp, the Jews and other "undesirables" were forced to give up all they had: their luggage, their clothes, every last belonging, be it sacred or quotidian. To add to the humiliation, the captors would take any gold teeth, strip all spectacles and detain all undergarments, and even the very hair from the prisoner's heads was removed.

The first room held holy artifacts, items that Jews, especially Orthodox Jews and Rabbis, held in great reverence. Behind thick glass I saw prayer shawls and holy writ that were instantly seized upon arrival. As others took note, and moved on, I stared at the blues and whites of intricately sewn religious garb, imagining the pain that the men must have felt when they were torn away from them in a ribald and heartless display of hate and thievery.

Being a religious person myself, with deep roots in Christian faith, I could empathize in the smallest degree. I had things that were holy to me, things that I wouldn't tolerate to be disrespected. And now I understood better than ever the grade of dehumanization in process in the concentration camps. Adjacent to this display was a smaller layout, with tiny dresses, bonnets, and baby shoes. This one tore me completely apart. I couldn't look at it very long without welling up with tears. Sure, it happened decades ago, but the imagination and the memory are powerful things, things that have the mysterious ability of bringing things into relevance, bringing dead things alive again. I stood there and held back tears for the mothers who would never see their infants again, and my stomach churned for the fathers that would never teach their kids how to throw a ball, or teach them anything for that matter. I thought of my own parents and the love that that they had woven into my life from day one. In the same way that you put yourself in the shoes of the protagonist in a dramatic movie, I put myself in the shoes of the family members that lost so much. I was reminded of the ingenious brevity of the author Thomas Wolfe who scattered his novel *Look Homeward, Angel* with the phrase "O Lost!" to describe a shifting world of loneliness and a life of misdirection and loss.

Again I had lagged behind, and had to jog to the next room that housed a prodigious number of ruthlessly pilfered items. Behind one glass wall were thousands upon thousands of pots and pans, dishes, cutlery, and other chipped pieces of enamelware. The broken paint and rusted metal rolled on in an endless heap of stolen contraband that the Nazis intended on using for the express purpose of making more bullets. More bloodshed.

To my right was another mountain of miscellaneous items that the S.S.[4] felt were unnecessary for camp life. These were amenities that the Jews had brought to the ghettos, usually whatever they could fit in one suitcase. Upon deportation to the "work camps" they were told to bring their personal affects. But the cruel intention of the guards to seize every possession of the prisoners was never in doubt. Asking the Jews to bring their things to the new camps only made the plundering thereof that much more painful. I saw shoe-shining kits, gloves, handkerchiefs, toiletries and other basic tools of existence that would never be seen again. Such simple items, items I took for granted every single day.

---

[4] *Shutzstaffel,* literally meaning protection squadron—a major paramilitary organization under Nazi regime.

We weaved through another corridor, making our way to a new room. This time the display case ran across the entire wall. Behind a veil to the past, the protective layer of glass, laid an array of antiquated prosthetics. There are certain things that most humans never entertain in their heads; they aren't unfathomable, just not things that would ever organically enter our brains. Seeing removed and purloined prosthetics from some seventy years ago, with their ancient materials and outdated uses, was one of those things. Strewn about on top of what appeared to be an endless white sheet were these crutches, prosthetic legs, archaic wheelchairs, and broken braces of thousands of innocent and disabled people. It was sickening to think of the Nazis stealing these necessities from the unsuspecting individuals, but the real sadness was in the messy truth. The truth was anyone with a supposed abnormality, disability, or ailment of any sort would be un-euphemistically disposed of. They would not have their crutches taken, and be forced to work whilst hobbling and limping, but they would have met a destiny far worse, ending in death and smoke, usually the first ones to be surreptitiously led away to the flames.

As if this was not enough weight upon my soul, we carried on to another set of conjoining rooms within the same brick building. This next pile of filched items was a hill of empty suitcases and wicker baskets. As I entered the room I felt as empty and hollow as those pieces of luggage behind the glass barrier. The Nazis had managed to vacuum up my energy years after their treachery. I saw the brown leathers and white markings of surnames that would not be passed on, legacies and traditions that would come to a sudden and cruel halt. In the middle of the jumbled mountain, the name Pasternak poked out, and beneath it laid the luggage of a Mr. Steindler. In the distance, barely visible, I saw Orov, a suitcase personified, protruding through the rubble, almost as if to say "Remember me?" A Mr. Greilsamer was dormant and silent. He was probably a father and a husband, probably a great man. I thought of my own surname and what it would look like on a discarded box of my own belongings. The whole idea of it all ripped my insides asunder. I shuffled on laterally and saw dozens more names, Slavic and Germanic names I couldn't pronounce. But I knew they all had a history, a past full of holidays, newborns, smiles and Bar mitzvahs. I would never know the exact contents of those suitcases, nor would anyone else, and for some reason that truly upset me.

The Germans euphemistically called the area where the seized items were sorted and stored "Canada." Hitler's minions would rummage through the belongings of tens of thousands of people in search of valuables and any salvageable piece of material that could somehow benefit the German cause. With endless avarice they would look for coins, earrings, heirlooms, and other items to satiate their greed. All the while those who were left with nothing were reduced to nothing, whether through starvation, emaciation, or through the dreaded ruddy brick chimneys.

All of the "Canadian" rooms seemed to melt together. Before I knew it I was in another room, verklempt beyond reason, looking horror dead in the face. This was one of the few places on the camp grounds that photography was prohibited, for preservation or reverence I knew not, but the solemnity of the room was unmistakable. This room was the room where the hair was kept.

The process of arriving in camp was always horrendous for the prisoners. It was an onslaught of humiliation and dehumanization with rifle butts and raging dogs moving the inmates from one area to another. An essential portion of "initiation" was the cutting of the pupil's hair. This was never done gingerly or with style; it was sheared off violently and haphazardly. Naked men and women were now bald, nearly scalped, and almost always with fresh cuts on their heads. Even the hair of children was cut before they were surreptitiously led to the gas chambers. Along with the desire to upset, disorient and debase their slaves, the Nazis used the hair to make mattresses. For being viewed as vermin, the Jews sure had a lot to offer the supreme race, even when they seemingly had nothing left to give. I stood and wondered, years later how many Nazi-made mattresses still dotted the homes of Europe, where innocent and delightful people slept.

At first glance, the sea of hair looked like a mysterious pile of refuse. It makes sense now, but never before had I seen so much hair thrown together in such an ugly and prodigious manner. People around me gasped audibly and talked in hushed and shocked tones. I stood paralyzed near the first few yards of hair. I saw rivers of brown locks, with occasional curls of blonde and black intertwined in the infinite heap. I looked more intently, searching for internal answers. As everyone else does, I asked myself, how could someone do this? How could this happen? I knew they were complex questions that weren't answerable with nice responses and glib remarks. But alas, I stood there and asked. A little faded blue ribbon was still holding together a pony tail that had been chopped off years and years ago. Withered hair ties and clips could be seen through the mess. Some of the hair I knew was that of a child, and that reality hit me like an unseen tackle from behind. I felt like getting on my knees and crying, but dozens of people milled around about me. I felt like I was having an extremely intimate and personal experience at noon in Central Park. Tears formed in my blinking eyes, and I let them come. This was not something I could ever unsee, and though it hurt, I wanted to take it in. I walked slowly and pondered a little longer than I felt was necessary and respectful.

We walked out into the sunlight, but I was still in a dark place. As my eyes had to adjust to the light, my mind would have to adjust from what I had just seen. And the tour was not even halfway through. It was time to enter Block 11. Block 11 was located at the far corner of the camp, adjacent to the famous Death Wall. Inside the block we walked through rooms of torture. Images of indescribable pain and unfettered screams bursted into my mind. We walked down the stairs into a dark corridor where punished inmates would be beaten and experimented on. A small cell was designated for certain offenses, where those who entered were forced to stand the entire night and then return to hard labor the following day. The cruelty of the Nazis seemed to know no bounds; it seemed to only increase as the tour progressed. Very little of what I saw in Auschwitz was new information for me, but it still struck me and affected me in a vivid way I was not expecting. It was like getting34161 hit by lightning. I am well aware of lightning and the potentially fatal surge of electricity it carries, but until I get hit by a bolt I will never really understand its power. Sure, I have been shocked before, and felt volts of electricity flow through my body, but to actually have lightning hit my body, leaving me singed, is a completely different beast.

Before heading to the crematoria, we walked briefly over to the Death Wall. Here countless victims were shot to death as a punitive consequence of whatever arbitrary misdemeanors the Nazis had contrived. It was a brick wall with an extra portion of concrete added to the part where bullets would fly, blood would spurt, and bones would shatter. It was a nondescript part of camp, placed conspicuously between two blocks. It seemed more holy and revered than most places within the camp, as it was surrounded by myriad bouquets of flowers, candles, small rocks of remembrance and other mournful paraphernalia. Some Asian tourists decked with expensive cameras and cheap sunglasses stepped in and out taking pictures and talking loudly. I took a moment to reflect on those who just a few feet away from me had looked at life for the last time. Against the wall, on the day of their execution, the Jews were ordered to face the wall. However, many refused, and demanded to look their killers in the eye before they perished. I don't know if I would have the courage to face my enemy head on, nor do I know if I would be capable of holding back tears, or screams for mercy and of desperation. We all like to think we would display great bravery and unmatched strength in times of chaos and horror, but there is no way to really know unless that ungodly day arrives. The truth is most of us would likely weep and wail, beg and prostrate in the most pathetic fashion.

# chapter 4

*"And then I cry. Because of the murder of the children? No, I don't know them. No, I cry because I, too, belong to the human race."*

~Konnilyn G. Feig

With a heavy heart I joined my group in heading toward the gas chambers. Just before we reached the crematoriums, we passed some gallows and the housing unit of the camp's sadistic commandant, Rudolph Hoss who was ironically hanged upon those very gallows, mere yards from his villa, an event subsequently immortalized in the closing scenes of *Schindler's List*. Two salient statements by Hoss give us an especially real insight into the terror and murder that he inflicted and oversaw. In an affidavit used in the Nuremberg Trials, Hoss callously comments on "improvements" the camp had made in contrast to the Treblinka camp:

> Still another improvement we made over Treblinka was that at Treblinka the victims almost always knew that they were to be exterminated and at Auschwitz we endeavoured to fool the victims into thinking that they were to go through a delousing process. Of course, frequently they realised our true intentions and we sometimes had riots and difficulties due to that fact. Very frequently women would hide their children under the clothes but of course when we found them we would send the children in to be exterminated.

To juxtapose this unrepentant admission of guilt, Hoss sent over a message to the state prosecutor just four days before his execution in an obvious attempt to elicit mercy and forgiveness for his heinous crimes. With a veneer of false remorse and insulting timing, he concludes his final dictation:

> My conscience compels me to make the following declaration. In the solitude of my prison cell I have come to the bitter recognition that I have sinned gravely against humanity. As Commandant of Auschwitz I was responsible for carrying out part of the cruel plans of the 'Third Reich' for human destruction. In so doing I have inflicted terrible wounds on humanity. I caused unspeakable suffering for the Polish people in particular. I am to pay for this with my life. May the Lord God forgive one day what I have done.

All of this death, coupled with thoughts of retribution and moral reciprocity, followed me past the gallows, the Nazi estates, and into the small entrance to what was the sole gas chamber of Auschwitz I.

This portion of the visit is impossible to prepare for. It is a visceral experience that transcends any amount of knowledge or mental toughness. The corridor that led to the gas chamber was narrow and dark. Noises echoed off the walls in incomprehensible cries, cries that bounced back in Russian, Polish, Yiddish and a dozen other tongues. I felt the same emptiness of the gut that you feel when you are about to speak in public; I could see the room ahead and already I could hear tourists around me crying. Some were reverently wiping away tears as they rolled down their cheeks, others gave no effort in masking the sounds of their pain. I couldn't blame them for their fervent outcry. The truth is, many men wish they could be more sensitive, wish they could do what their hearts desired, but what appears outwardly less masculine. Brenda Ueland spoke of this squelched passion saying, "Men spend their lives adding and subtracting and dictating letters when they secretly long to write sonnets and play the violin and burst into tears at the sunset." I didn't want to weep at the mere sight of a descending sun, but I oft times wished a fallen tear wasn't viewed as a sign of weakness. Something about those closed-in walls, the darkness and the pain made me realize a potential depth within myself, and seeing others openly demonstrate their emotions was beautiful and encouraging.

The wall to my right was black and grimy. About seven feet up the decaying wall were visible scratch marks, a most gruesome and terrifying vestige that left me spooked and uncomfortable. I reached up and touched them with my hand, feeling the fingernail marks from decades past, the last bodily movement of many, an extant testament that the human body will instinctively fight until the last breath.

I wanted to take pictures, but I wanted to be fully present in the moment. My sister to my left grabbed my arm and cried like she had just witnessed what history was currently showing us. A single vase filled with red and white flowers lay in the middle of the room behind the ropes that separated the crowd, and directly below where the Zyklon B[5] gas was administered through a little door in the ceiling. Next to the vase lay a small ignited ivory colored candle. The flowers spoke in tones of silent hope. The redness of the petals grabbed me and shot images of blood and carnage into my head. The contrast of white symbolized to me the safe haven of an afterlife, whatever the victims believed; any celestial home would be better than the reality they had known. The colors and images were beautiful and horrifying.

    I reluctantly moved into the conjoining room to the left, making sure to notice the intricacies of the Third Reich architecture. I wanted to understand, as much as I could, the diabolical plan of the Nazis. But again, I was stupefied as I stared at the ovens. These were giant cooking machines specifically designed to cremate and obliterate the bodies of the innocent that were mercilessly asphyxiated in the adjacent room. The ovens were large with obvious doors in the front where naked corpses would be quickly and violently shoved in,

---

[5] Translated as Cyclone B, a cyanide-based pesticide invented in Germany in the early 1920's.

usually by the hands of those who would soon take their place, joining them in whatever heaven might lay ahead.

The room was fittingly absent of light, lit only by a lone lightbulb and the fleeting screens of cellphones and digital cameras. The ovens were aged and stained with soot, the black smoke of the dead. The ceiling was low, and the ground was concrete just like the walls. Every step of Auschwitz felt like prison, and that was the design and desire of Hitler's evil blueprints.

My stomach felt uneasy as we made our way out of the room and back outside in view of the commandant's villa. The gas chamber was appropriately the last stop for us at Auschwitz I, as it was for millions before us. As sick as I felt, I got to leave on my two feet. I got to get on an air-conditioned bus and move on with my life. I would see the sunrise again, and I would see and love my family once again. The chambers were eerily sinister, but they gave me immediate perspective, reminding me of how blessed my seemingly unremarkable life was.

We walked as a big group back to the entrance of camp to return our headsets and carry on to Auschwitz II-Birkenau. Most everyone hustled back to the gate a few hundred yards away. Not me. I walked in pensive slowness, looking at the now powerless electric fences and the signs warning of their lethal voltage in angry German, accompanied by a skull with penetrating, evil eyes.

I thought of how alone I felt at times, how unwanted and undesired I could feel. But these I could now see were figments of a flawed imagination, an imagination molded by my culture and surroundings. I wasn't alone, not truly, and I never had been. Sure, I had felt down and unimportant before, just like everyone else. But true despondency, true aloneness, true rejection and dehumanization, I had never felt. Again, Auschwitz had reminded me how loved and unlonely I truly was.

As I neared the entrance point I took one last look at a world that was once a ground for systematic killing. My heart ached to think people in such a recent time could be so terrible, so ruthless. I wondered how awful it would be to take all of this in as a person of Jewish heritage. Again my heart seemed to slide down my chest and I turned away with a prayer in my heart for better times and for the ability to forgive.

I got back on the bus, headed to the back and sat down, thumbing through the book I had purchased and looking through the hundreds of pictures I had taken on my phone. There was an irreverence of noise and idle chatter amongst the other passengers that I resented. I couldn't understand their callousness. In my mind, we were simply going from one holy place to another, from Auschwitz I, to Auschwitz II-Birkenau. Most acted like we were taking a quick break between carnival rides.

The feeling of this camp was similar to the first, but seemed less like a field trip. There were fewer tourists, less noise, and more to see, more destruction, more expansion. Through the arched entrance almost the entire camp was visible, or at least the view was unobstructed by brick and mortar. As far as I could see were fields of well-manicured grass, old housing barracks and the strangled echoes of death.

We received a new tour guide, another stout female of ambiguous European descent, but this tour was marked with a more punctuated intimacy. There were only a few other groups walking about, and it was much easier here to spread out, to avoid clogged lines, and there were fewer sorry attempts to hush voices. Right through the bricked arches my feet took me, and I instantly took in the vastness of the complex, all the while struggling with the complexity of it all.

There was an ineffable aroma of nothingness, an eternal feeling of emptiness. We followed the line of the defunct train tracks with remnants of a terribly real past on my left, disease and destruction on my right. Though, what was the difference between the two sides? Both held death, both sides lay dormant behind a seemingly endless array of barbed wire fencing. Both sides were encircled by grass and near dirt paths. Had it been winter, mud and snow would have been the main attractions, but in the glory of June the sun was a rose in a swamp, a light in a deep and obscure cave.

Our group trudged forward towards the four crematoria, stopping periodically to hear brief and overly simplistic explanations of history and our surroundings. I couldn't be bothered to listen for the most part. I wanted to be alone with my thoughts, no matter how tortured they were. I wanted to be the only person in that black camp, there, alone with my existential ponderings. As is the case for everyone who visits Auschwitz or any of the other "camps," the same internal questions prevail: Why did this happen? How could this happen? An infinite stream of "whys" invade your conscience, even though you know the answers are not simple, and you know they will not ease your pain or satiate your morbid curiosity into the human psyche. They are complicated answers that will never fully be answered, and will never truly satisfy a visitor attempting to understand, desperately trying to know. But when you are "visiting" a death camp, you transform into much more than a mere visitor or observer. You are no longer just a student or tourist; you enter into the core of human history and look it square in the tearful, bloodshot eye. Perhaps this is not the experience of all who visit the camps scattered across Europe, but for me the verb *visit* does not suffice. It seems too contradicting. Does the word *visit* not conjure up thoughts of welcoming, thoughts of leisure and vacation, the very antithesis of the Holocaust?

Halfway to the pile of rubble that was Crematorium IV was a cattle car just to the side of the railroad tracks. It was one of the only remaining rail cars that had brought prisoners into the camp. Like wild animals, they were ushered out by screaming Germans, ravenous dogs, and a most unwelcoming stench. Dehydrated, emaciated, and undoubtedly covered in their own excrement, the frightened prisoners filed out and were shown their place in the living graveyard.

The boxcar had barely visible red paint and a little dedicatory plaque commemorating those who had passed. I took it in briefly, then returned to the track. I lay down in the middle of the track on my stomach and looked sadly towards the entrance. As I would repeatedly do throughout the camp, I tried to put myself in the shoes of those who had come before me. It was an impossible task, but I came closer having tried, having stopped, and having opened up my mind in a vacuous attempt to feel what was felt. The human mind and body are incredible things, but it is impossible to truly walk in another's shoes, to truly understand another's plight or to truly know what another has gone through. But we can open our hearts and inch closer, and if nothing else we are left with empathy and a new love, a love we had previously known nothing about.

There was a disconnect. Teenagers around me sat on the dirt complaining of the long day and the hours without cellphone service. I was nauseated by what I heard and the irreverence of those thoughtless youths who were lucky enough to walk long distances and have nearly constant access to cellular communication. I silently wished that these types would just stay home and experience history via YouTube.

I took a few pictures low to the ground with dirt all over my pants and pebbles piercing my arms. The shots were stark and beautiful, a strange, inexplicable beauty.

I got up and hustled up to our group that was nearing the infamous Crematorium IV, the gas chamber that was destroyed with explosives by the very Jews that were doomed to die within the walls. This killing center was at the far end of the camp, past the end of the train tracks, off the dirt path, and through some grassy trails. All that was left was a roped off heap of crumbled concrete, corroded rebar, and dark red brick strewn about in an organized mess. Birch trees surrounded the mass graves as silent sentinels, muted witnesses to the horror of burned bodies and endless sadism. I didn't know if any of the trees within my sight had been there since WWII, but I obsessively wondered. How sad and poetic would it be if the only surviving witnesses of the sabotage and carnage at Crematorium IV were innocent and unsuspecting birch trees? The irony for my wild mind was in the fact that those trees could surely produce paper, and upon paper could be written the sins of the Nazis, but tragically, trees cannot write. They do however, give us oxygen, another thing those in the gassed room could have used. It was a strange stream of thoughts, but it disturbed and intrigued me nonetheless.

Though it is a sad and awful reminder of Nazi crimes, Crematorium IV is a rather romantic place now, with the trappings of historical mystery and intrigue. I am sure many would disagree with my assessment of what would constitute a romantic vestige of history, but knowing what was left behind and what this center of death symbolizes rather awakens my soul.

Few survived the explosion of Crematorium IV, but those who did attested its existence to the world. Buried beneath the earth are hand-written accounts of camp life, placed there by walking corpses desperate for one last chance to share their story. They knew that surviving the conditions of Auschwitz were bleak, and living through the war, if it ever ended, seemed a blissful impossibility. So, they boldly and surreptitiously left time capsules beneath the feet of killers and below the smoke and ash of loved ones. Their wild hope was that if they couldn't retell the horror they experienced, it would be read and the culpability of the Germans would be undeniable. As we know, the chimneys came falling down in a blaze of gunfire and explosive crashing. The witnesses for the most part were executed, but quietly beneath bloody soil remain those revealing documents.

Fast forward to present day; aren't we blessed to be able to have those personal accounts left behind for our knowledge and scholarship? Well, if only it were that simple. Jewish tradition ironically makes retrieving these lost memoirs impossible. Here's why: Judaic law dictates that a Jewish grave should not be disturbed under any circumstance. It may not be moved, renovated, or altered in any fashion. Exhumations are unthinkable, and examination for historical inquiry is likewise prohibited. So, though countless historians and descendants of those murdered at Auschwitz want to dig beneath the rubble and find those stories, those heartbreaking accounts, the respect for the wishes of the Jewish community is understandably prioritized.

So, as I stood inches from the debris, I couldn't help but wonder how close I stood to undiscovered, priceless historical documents. They could be right under my feet, a worm's house away or they could be deep beneath the holy ground far from where I rested. The curiosity as a historian was torturing me, but as a person I also longed to know more, I longed to read what was currently unreadable. Though it was a depressing place to stand, the mystery and allure of those eyewitness accounts brutally captivated me.

Birds flew by unaware of the hallowed grounds and chirped their songs happily oblivious. I would not be as lucky as those flying creatures. They would never understand the purview of hate and evil that permeated the earth, a hate that was supremely evident just below their nests. I envied their innocence and their inability to destroy their own kind. Many animals are ravenous killers, and bloodthirsty, but never without utility, and never would they be capable of complete genocide. Only man could do this.

I could have stayed in that very spot the rest of the afternoon, consumed in thought and prayer, but the group quickly and loudly moved onward. We walked away and came upon a huge memorial, an artistic piece of light harnessed in a jungle of darkness. The enormous stone monuments brought a smile to my face. People had dedicated their lives to making sure the Holocaust was not forgotten, and if nothing else to pay homage to the millions whose lives were stolen. That kind of humanity is why studying the Holocaust is not a depressing matter, for as much wickedness and turmoil is found in books, films, and museums concerning the Holocaust, there is always another side, perhaps not a smiling gleeful side, but a hopeful, humane side in contrast.

To our right was Crematorium III, not quite as destroyed as Crematorium IV, but still in ruins. Our tour was coming to an end, so we simply stopped from a distance and took pictures. Many in our group were wholly uninterested with yet another destroyed building. Their continual lack of respect and appreciation maddened me, but I was not going to be negatively affected.

We passed the broken chimneys and fallen structures and made our way back to the beginning of the camp for the final portion of the visit, exploring the living quarters, the barracks. It was hot and I was tired, but as we moved past watchtowers and endless rows of destroyed buildings and bygone housing units, I could see perfectly in my head thousands of starving inmates digging trenches, sweating and crying. I could see people fainting from exhaustion and people crazily scratching their lice-ridden bodies. I watched as people soiled themselves and writhed in pain. This was all in my imagination, but it was a reality, and the realness of Auschwitz was getting to me. It was as if the place was haunted, but not like a spooky old house on the bayou. I didn't feel like ghosts were trying to scare me or harm me, but I could feel the coldness of death, and the ground seemed to almost quake with the voices of millions. It was confusing and overwhelming, but again I felt silly and guilty for even thinking I was tired or hot.

The living barracks were hard to see. I knew what I was getting into. Some of the most famous and frequently seen photos are from the liberation of Auschwitz, and the photographs within the barracks. But photos cannot prepare you for physically being there.

The wooden barracks at Birkenau resembled shoddy barns with lower ceilings. In fact, they were designed for the housing of forty-eight horses. But each barrack held up to 800 people. The first barrack we entered was immediately hushed by our tour guide. I had ignored her for the majority of the camp, but now in closer quarters it was time to listen. She told us how each bunk, being about the size of a single bed, would have three people crammed in it at night. Sleeping at night, though a much needed respite from long and violent work days, was not all that pleasant. The close quarters made the spread of disease inevitable. The only real solace was in the body heat and the time off their feet, and away from the sadistic S.S. officers. Lice had the largest population of the whole camp, and would jump from one victim to another in the cold and unforgiving night. Oh the awful images that came to me. Though it was hot outside, the barracks felt cold. The concrete ground was stained with black grime and whispers from the past.

The next barrack we entered was identical from the outside and appeared to have the same square footage and design inside, looking much like a drab barn. But this barn did not have any sort of bedding, or concrete posts holding things up. This was the camp latrine. Down the middle there was a clearing, a walkway of sorts, while on the right and left sides there was a long row of latrines, and a third row after another pathway. The preserved privies were concrete structures about as high as my knees and were nothing more than enormous slabs of concrete with basketball-sized holes cut out. The rows of "toilets" resembled some strange and boring piece of modern art, one of those public displays that makes no sense to you, but is meant to provoke deep thought and wonderment. The holes that were clearly used as receptacles for human waste were made so close together that if two people were using adjacent holes it would be impossible for their bodies not to touch unless they were both small children. I thought how humiliating it would have been to relieve myself in such a public way, how utterly mortified I would have been as my bare skin was sandwiched between three or four strangers. As I was toying with the gruesome possibility in my head, our tour guide informed us that at any given time the latrine would have around 2,000 people inside vying for places to empty their bowels. I looked around and tried to count how many holes there were. I think there were around 180 exact places to go to the bathroom besides the ground. I may have been off, but there could not have been more than 200. As I finished counting, my stomach churned just in time to hear our guide say that in Birkenau it was impossible to visit the latrine without getting human feces spackled on you. Not only was the number of inmates in one facility ridiculously high, but nearly every prisoner suffered from violent diarrhea. It wasn't just an embarrassing moment, defecating in front of thousands of people; it was the vilest and most degrading experience. It was a disgusting, putrid sort of chaos. It was yet another ugly child of war. The stench must have been unbearably nauseating. With my quick gag reflex I wouldn't have been able to go to the bathroom without vomiting. As sick as these thoughts were, I imagined how terrible it would be to attempt to throw up in a hole covered in excrement. Having my face near it all would have only fueled further hurling.

      I thought I appreciated porcelain toilets and first world plumbing when I returned from living in South America for two years. But the outhouses of Brazil were nothing compared to the horror of Auschwitz. My legs felt heavy. I started to think of all the times that I had complained of unsatisfactory toilet paper, or voiced my displeasure in sitting on such a cold surface early in the morning. What wicked and selfish thoughts. The inmates of Auschwitz had nothing but their own prison garb and anything else they could scrounge around camp as toilet paper. They never had to deal with chilly porcelain seats, but the freezing Polish winters would leave soiled remains frozen on the ground and on the very spot where business was had. Comparisons cannot really be made. Our mind naturally compares our own experience, our own trials, with what we are seeing or hearing, but there is no real comparison.

I stood amazed and bewildered, disturbed and upset like I had just seen a snake devour a baby deer. Right in front of me stood a young man with his arms folded. He was only a foot away from the grand procession of latrines. He just stared down in quiet disbelief. To the left of me stood a robust woman in her thirties, with a sad and ruddy complexion. She stood alone with her hands resting on her stomach, staring across the room, staring, but not looking at anything in particular. She was deep in thought, but could not bring herself to look down. On the other side of the giant room were three elderly Japanese men with khaki pants, dark blazers and sun deflecting hats. They looked away and shook their heads, muttering something softly and tersely. We walked out and I couldn't believe it.

This barrack concluded our tour of the Auschwitz-Birkenau Concentration Camp. I headed back to the entrance on the dirt path, taking one last look at the terrible vista from a place I would likely never stand again. My sister called me over, back near the barrack to take a picture with me. Now, posing for pictures at Auschwitz is a moral conundrum in itself. Does one smile? Surely a frown isn't obligatory, but a smirk or an especially toothy grin seems inappropriate. But, as always, you want to convey the moment. You want the photograph to remind you years later what you felt as it was being taken. And though my heart was weighed down and my soul was tired and bothered, I was happy. I felt blessed to be there, and I felt blessed for all the things I would never have to endure. I put my arm around my beautiful twenty-nine year old sister and smiled a sort of toothless half smile. Brittany on the other hand looked like she just got off a sinuous rollercoaster. Her shoulders sunk and her face revealed a deep and unanswered melancholy. I guess that's how she felt. I teased her for donning a "raging frown," but I couldn't blame her. Visiting Auschwitz reveals many of the same emotions and ethical questions as a funeral does for someone who has never attended one before.

    While others in our group took pictures, I leaned against a wooden post and gazed into the distance of Birkenau. I looked through the wired fencing into the grassy fields without a discernible thought in my head. Or maybe my thoughts were so rapid and complex that I could not decipher one from the other. I looked at a group of teenage girls laughing and taking pictures. Some of them smiled, hand on their hips, like they were posing for a homecoming picture. Others clearly struggled to land the appropriate smile. This time their frivolity paid me no bother. The tour was over, and I was just feeling blessed. I felt light again. It was a confusing sort of felicity, but it felt apropos to the moment.

The group scurried out of the facility, snapping last minute photos and talking loudly. I lagged behind with a most affable woman from North Carolina. She was a high school history teacher and appreciated the camp the way I felt everyone should. Her accent was strong, but left no room for doubting her intellect. Her sentences were long, but always contained a strong and surprisingly relevant point. Her name was Teresa, and God knows somewhere far from me she had a full and beautiful life. We conversed all the way back to the bus, stopping frequently to take pictures through the weeds. The sun had changed its location, and the sky elicited a different canvas than it had on the walk in. I was the last to board the bus. I sat down, feeling a sense of completion as if I had just finished some great physical feat. My thoughts funneled out the window, and we drove towards Krakow.

# chapter 5

*"If we climb high enough, we will reach a height from which tragedy ceases to look tragic."*

~Irvin D. Yalom

The hilly drive from Oświęcim to Krakow is bucolic and easy on the senses. Small homes are scattered about the land with smoking chimneys and working farmers. It seemed like these tiny towns we zoomed past were completely unaware of the rest of the world. Time had frozen over this forgotten region. The sky was clear and the simple beauty of the countryside was starting to move me. Rural Poland rolled past, filled with idyllic homes and gorgeous sunsets. Perhaps it was a paltry and dreary place to pass through, but the romance of a never before seen land, a spot on the map unknown to most of the human race, entranced me. Still, the horror and reality of Auschwitz remained so near. I wondered if the locals were bothered by the truth and history of their geography.

In quaint European villages families tend to stay in one home for the span of their lives unless they are forced out for some reason. Surely there was an old grandfather or dying widow that still lived close by, with stark and vivid recollections of WWII and its atrocities. I wanted to leap off the bus and talk to the locals, but we had a tight schedule and I knew not a word of Polish.

Fields of green passed by and my eyes got heavy. We were approaching our next great city. Church steeples poked through the trees in the distance and an old castle displayed its stony head out on top of a hill not far off. All of the sudden we were in the old city. I guess when you are accustomed to American cities, any European city seems antiquated and excitingly enigmatic. Soviet era apartment complexes popped up like sad giant cinderblocks. Amid the broken windows and graffiti were Catholic churches, and hidden restaurants. Bridges, trolleys, and people teemed about the streets as we travelled through alleyways, and twisted behind tall trees and a darkening sky. Just 66 kilometers away from the chimneys and the gallows and we were in a different world. The contrast was tremendous. The prick of Auschwitz's thorn still left my soul throbbing, but just like a child forgets about his cut knee if you pinch his arm, the pain and weariness I had felt left for a season, my senses now dominated by a lighter place. The heaviness of my thoughts had temporarily subsided as I walked the enchanting streets of Krakow. But like the scraped child, my wound would need additional healing once I forgot that I had been pinched.

    The next day and a half I roamed the streets of Krakow, breathing in the architecture and culture of one of the oldest cities in Poland. I walked up to the edge of the Vistula River, and entered giant cathedrals that I'll never forget. I ate beet soup with hard-boiled eggs and got lost for the better part of three hours. All the church steeples led me to believe I always knew where I was, but in reality they only confused my already poor sense of direction. I drank lukewarm Coke and envisioned a life in that beautiful city. Perhaps the University of

Krakow could be my new home. The women were brilliantly put together, and the language was one I felt I could pick up. It wasn't rational or remotely pragmatic thinking, but I seriously weighed the options in my head. I was so disenchanted with America that becoming a Cracovian sounded amazing. I didn't have much in my bank account, no real job, no girlfriend, no girl that made me surge with poetry and endless lust. So why go home? What was left to be desired in the States?

    The last two days of my trip were spent in Prague, or rather Praha, as it is known by the Czech people. Once the capital of the Holy Roman Empire, Praha was an artist's paradise. The bridges stretched out over sparkling tribunes and Gothic churches shimmered in the distance. Street artisans drew intricate pictures of gargoyles and unknowing strangers. The city smelled like a fairy tale. I felt instantly imbued with literary inspiration. I sat on the Charles Bridge and wrote for hours, dreaming of my life back home, and the life I wanted to create. My pen seemed faster and more acute than before, more keen to its surroundings and to its purpose as a tool of words, a constructer of sentences. I knew writers loved Paris and London for their romantic appeal. But I thought it was just an excuse to abandon their lives, their failed relationships, and to write about eating baguettes. But there was something about a city with so much history, so much culture, so much bustling. It seemed to crack open corners of the brain that had never been opened. My last days in Europe were sad, sad because I wanted more. I felt like I had never tasted salt before and someone gave me one potato chip. It was eternally inadequate. So, I said goodbye to the Czech Republic and a reluctant adieu to Western Europe. I had slept little on the trip, so a little rest on the airplane sounded glorious. The bus ride to the airport was disheartening. Buildings and street signs with too many consonants whizzed by and I wondered if I would see any of them ever again.

    I would also never see that blonde again, that blonde that worked in the hotel bar. I asked her where some good restaurants in town were just so I could talk to her. Her English was slow and broken, but her face was a Da Vinci painting come to life. She was flawless and now gone forever. Curse the romantic inside me that refused to capitulate. Alas, it was time to go home. We arrived at the airport and I said goodbye to Daniel, our brilliant tour guide. Daniel was fluent in five languages and though being thirty-nine, looked no older than twenty-eight. His German accent was warm and comforting, his humor and intellect would remain with me. Daniel was kind and talkative, but just distant enough not to get attached. Touring and knowledge were his life. I envied his life of travel, and empathized with the loneliness I knew he felt.

I got my final European treats for the flight and boarded with reticence and wonder in my heart. I hoped one day I could return, with more money and an even different perspective on life and tragedy. But who knows what the future will bring. Maybe I would travel greatly, or perhaps a sickness would impede my whimsy, perhaps a lover would hold me back, or maybe I would utter those sad words year after year: "Someday I will go back."

I sat down and quickly ate all my uniquely European potato chips and candies. I put in headphones and attempted to read. But the words were nothing more than something seen, they could not stick in my brain. I was feeling too much to attempt to feel something else. It was like when I was waiting night after night in the hospital hoping my grandfather would recover from his heart surgery and come back to us. I stayed up through the night with my dad so my grandma and mom could sleep, but also so someone was present at all times in the ICU in case the doctors had bad news for us. I brought snacks and books, but I could not read. I attempted to read a volume of letters written between two famous poets. But I just kept re-reading stanzas and glossing over paragraphs. I gave up quickly. How could I escape into the life of another, when the life of my grandpa, the man who taught me how to ride a horse, who sang loudly every morning of his life, was slipping away just down the hall? I could not. It felt too insensitive. My grandpa was a beautiful man, austere and gentle, and he deserved better. Even though I needed some menial distraction, reading could not be it. And though this long airplane ride back to Salt Lake City was not very similar to my heart pummeling experience in that hospital, just like that day I could not focus on the meanings of words, and I just wanted to stay in my own universe, rather than enter another's.

    I really don't remember much else about the flight. I remember our layover in JFK, and my immediate need to eat a Wendy's sandwich and resume my normal cellphone service. By the time we landed in Utah and I drove back to my apartment, I had no idea what day it was or when I would need breakfast, or dinner again. I walked into my room, stripped down and collapsed on my bed. I was exhausted. It wasn't just jet lag, or sleep deprivation. It was also a decrease in mental fortitude. I felt like all I had learned, all I had seen, and all I had been a part of had left me tired and weak. On my desk were overdue bills, and as I connected to the Wi-Fi, texts surged in, reminding me of my annoyingly modern life.

# chapter 6

*"We felt the need to understand"*

~Elie Wiesel

What compels a guy like me to study the Holocaust? I am a white Christian in his mid-twenties, with no ties to Judaism. I am a Gentile that doesn't know Hebrew, and has never been to Israel. But does my lack of association with the Jewish world preclude me from venturing into Holocaust studies? Does it make me an odd candidate for someone wanting to better understand and identify with Jews? Perhaps it does, but wait. Am I not a participant in the human experience? I am a student of history. I am a student of the past. I read voraciously about various cultures, ethnicities, and geopolitical issues. Yet I am frequently asked why I would want to study the Holocaust. This question is often followed with the sub-question, "Did you have a relative in the concentration camps?" Nope. All of my ancestors believed the Messiah had already come and were either already in America or in Ireland minding their own business when Hitler was raging across Europe. So where did my incongruous interest in the concentration camps and the Shoah stem? Well, it is difficult to pinpoint exactly why something grips you, and perhaps even more troubling to know the precise moment that interest was born.

My first memory of coming across Holocaust literature was when I was ten years old. My Mom and I were at Costco and I was looking at the books. I had yet to arrive at my true love of reading, so I was looking through the bigger books with interesting photographs. I flipped though *The*

*Guinness Book of World Records*, *Ripley's Believe it or Not*!, and other historic books in search of interesting facts and unknown stories. I saw another book to the side with fewer copies in the stack. I don't remember the title, but I saw the word Holocaust printed on the front in white letters, and the black and white face of a small child, clearly the victim of something. I had heard the word Holocaust before, and had a vague knowledge of its tie to World War II and Adolf Hitler, but I knew little more than that. I remember those eyes. The eyes of a little girl spoke to me, telling me to open the book and discover. I ignored the text and looked in awe at the black and white pictures of human beings barely hanging on to life. My eyes rushed from page to page in disbelief of the apparent torture and starvation in the concentration camps. I couldn't believe how emaciated the bodies were. I saw heaps of dead bodies and felt gross inside. I didn't fully understand. I knew war left many dead, and I knew that it wasn't pretty, but what these glossy pages showed me left me in a thick cloud of confusion. The book was expensive. But I had to have it. Maybe the accompanying text would make some sense of the horror. Whatever the price was, my mom wasn't going to spring for it. As always I could do some extracurricular choirs and save up some money with time. I decided to do that. That big maroon and white book had to be mine. But I got distracted. I was too busy practicing my left-handed layups and watching *Saved By The Bell* to try and gain a little extra cash. Fifteen years later I am distracted by the exact same things, sports and syndicated television shows. And my bank account is not that different from the days when all my money remained in a Ziploc bag under my bed.

Although I still wanted that book, and looked at it a few more times on other trips to Costco, I more or less forgot about it. As the years of my adolescence passed by swimmingly, my interest in global issues and historic events increased greatly. But my intrigue with the Holocaust was not really shaped until I read *Night* by Elie Wiesel my senior year in high school. My brusque mustached English teacher had lent me his copy of the book since I was unsatisfied with the books on the syllabus. He was the only teacher I ever remember crying in a lesson. The man had passion, and made us want to be passionate too. At that age you aren't sure what you want to be passionate about, but when you see it in an adult that you truly and secretly admire it makes you want to have fire inside of you. Charles Bukowski knows what I am talking about. He said, "Unless the sun inside you is burning your gut, don't do it." At seventeen it is wildly difficult to fully understand healthy obsessions, but seeing that bright yellow spark in another person helps.

I took that small book home and finished it in just a couple days. Little did I know that it had won the Nobel Peace Prize before I was even born.

All I knew was that it described another world, a terrible world that disturbed me. But for some reason I wanted to know more about that world, maybe to make more sense of it. Those 109 pages forever changed me. Some people were changed the first time they heard Fleetwood Mac or Nirvana, some were changed infinitely the summer they visited India, and others were forever altered after reading *Gone With The Wind*, but I was unequivocally changed after I read that tiny masterpiece. I looked at the human race in a different way. I was suddenly more aware of the power and presence of evil. I also realized how easy and unobtrusive my life had been.

I was now acutely aware of how little I knew about Europe, what little I understood of WWII, and how painfully obtuse I was about the Jewish people. Over the next few years of my life I read more books than I had previously read in my entire life up to that point. I procured more books about the Holocaust, and realized, as is the case with any area of study, that the more I learned, the more I wanted to know, and the more uneducated I ultimately felt.

I read more complex volumes on the matter, and even took an upper level anti-Semitism class my sophomore year of college. My interest was now getting intense. Any book remotely related to Nazism, Judaism, or European Jewry, I had to read. I was still naively unaware of the ocean of works that existed on the matter, and I was especially unaware of the many important tomes not yet translated into English.

I decided that one day when I was old and could afford it, I would journey to Europe and visit the camps. It was a bit of a pipe dream, but I decided definitively that if I travelled anywhere, it would be to Auschwitz. I had no idea that that opportunity would stroll into my life as soon as it did.

I hadn't started writing with any level of seriousness, but I knew I wanted to write about the Holocaust. I had no particular historical insight, but I felt like nothing gripped at the human experience from so many angles as the Holocaust did. I wrote papers about the invasion of Poland, and wrote extensively on Holocaust theory. But it was all very academic. Nothing new and revelatory. I wanted more. I wanted to meet survivors. I wanted to add to the wealth of research on the subject. I wanted to discover something, and share that with the world. I became obsessed with this idea, but struggled to finish my degree. I had student loans piling up and other financial issues that were making my dreams of becoming a historian less than likely, at least anytime in the near future.

But I kept studying and ran into several glimpses of hope. The first one was an idea for a book, an idea given to me on a silver platter by a friend who was fluent in German and loved history. Having lived in Germany for a couple years, he had learned of a specific underground plot to assassinate Hitler. It was called the Bavarian Freedom Initiative, or at least that is the closest translation from the more accurate German title, *Freiheitsaktion Bayern.* My friend Greg was excited about exploring this topic with his history major friend who happened to be a broke freelance writer as well. I was thrilled with the idea of researching a piece of history that had little light shed on it so far. It wasn't exactly Holocaust studies, but it was related to Germany and Hitler, so I was satisfied. I got ambitious, hitting the university library, scouring for anything related to this underground attempt to overthrow the great villain of Europe. But I found nothing. After countless Google searches and endless pestering of the librarian I decided to meet with a professor of German history. He would have to have some answers on where to turn with my overzealous and misguided enthusiasm. This professor, whose name I do not remember, was kind enough to meet with me in his stereotypically cluttered office. He asked about my project and my plans for research. He even admitted that he had not heard of this failed attempt to murder the Fuhrer. He offered me some advice that broke my heart ever so abruptly. This large man with dark grey hair told me in the most unambiguous way that I should not attempt to seriously study the Holocaust unless I planned on learning German. He added with a puff of arrogance that learning Hebrew, Polish, and Yiddish would not be a bad idea either. I thanked him for his obviously precious time and left his tiny office deflated. Maybe he was right. How much could I learn about a subject, when the majority of primary sources were written in a language I did not know? I couldn't write a whole book off of knowledge I had gleaned from Wikipedia.

While defeated, I realized Mr. Academia had a point. I wasn't ready to learn German. But maybe there were other portions of the Holocaust I could study deeply without the necessity of archives and umlauts.

A couple years passed and I still hadn't graduated college. I was focusing on coaching junior varsity basketball and making money. In my spare time, I probably read more than most full-time students, and none of my books had love stories or flying warlocks in them. I was reaching a point where I could say I knew more about the Holocaust than any other thing in the world, besides maybe basketball.

My second glimmer of hope came right after I finished a book about a Holocaust Survivor called *A Lucky Child*. As most first-hand accounts within Holocaust literature have deceased persons as authors, I was excited to read that this writer was still alive and well, teaching, and accepting e-mails. I sent Mr. Buergenthal a brief e-mail that I assumed would go unanswered. I sent him the following correspondence:

> Dear Professor Buergenthal, my name is Taylor Church and I am a history major at Utah Valley University where I will soon graduate and go on to pursue a career in teaching and writing. I just finished your book *A Lucky Child*. I absolutely loved it. I am sure you are an uber busy individual, so I will attempt to be brief. I was very disappointed that there is no English version of *Tommy* ever published. I was wondering if there is any way you would be interested in publishing the one copy you have for the world to read. Or if you would permit me to work on a subsequent translation from Norwegian into English, perhaps with supplementary history on the Sachsenhausen camp. I think this could be a beautiful project with many possible angles. Please let me know if this is in any way a possibility. Your book, like the many other Holocaust books I have read moved me in a most poignant way. I only hope that others could be so moved for the better with the possible release of the *Tommy* manuscript in English. Thank you.

I was thrilled with the swift response I received from a very busy octogenarian. He replied with the ingratiating words:

Dear Taylor Church,

Many thanks for your email and your kind words about my book. As for *Tommy*, it is now being translated into Norwegian by Mrs. Irene Levin Berman (see above email). I was told that the earlier translation was very poor.

Best regards,

Thomas Buergenthal

My hopes of creating a book about the Holocaust out of thin air were again foiled. But I didn't care. I actually spoke with a survivor of the camps. I exchanged pleasantries with a living hero, a symbol of the prevailing power of good versus evil. To many he was probably just a boring professor of comparative law and jurisprudence, but I found him to be a beacon of greatness and nobility.

Six months later I stumbled across another opportunity for a project. As none of my ideas had come to any sort of fruition, I was not expecting much. But the idea of discovering and in some way contributing to a sacred body of works excited me.

I think serendipity plays a major role in literary muses. It is easy to meander around waiting for beautiful ideas and an endless flow of great prose to arrive at your creative porch, but more often than not it comes in an unpredictable and untimely manner. It just requires a certain amount of observation and readiness. Orson Scott Card said, "Everybody walks past a thousand story ideas every day. The good writers are the ones who see five or six of them. Most people don't see any." So I guess the ability or chance of seeing an idea here or there, to me, is serendipity, for even if the idea becomes halted and unrealized, it will often lead to another greater idea or creative notion down the road.

I had just seen the movie *Into The Wild*, a true story about a young man who took to living alone in the wilderness of Alaska. The story tells a sad tale of loneliness, survival, and untimely death. After watching it, I was intrigued by an online article about the main character and his early death. It was an academic piece focusing on the plants that supposedly poisoned him, causing his death. The book and subsequent film are rather ambiguous in portraying the true cause of death. Over the years critics have speculated as to whether the death of Christopher McCandless was self-inflicted, starvation, or a death caused by the poison in the local flora that Christopher was forced to eat.

Years of scientific study and speculation have obviously brought about different schools of thought, but what this online article posited was that the poisonous plant that was guilty of murdering an innocent man was the same source of fodder that was fed to the inmates of an obscure concentration camp in Ukraine called Vapniarka. Now in years of studying the Holocaust and in its many aspects, I had never heard nor read the name Vapniarka. I realized there were thousands[6] of lesser camps that got lost in the sea of tragedy, obfuscated by camps with greater death tolls and more detailed histories. But the idea of writing a full length book on a camp that seemingly had nothing but a few articles and allusions to cover its history excited me terribly.

I immediately started what could, in my mind, eventually become a book or doctoral thesis. I knew it would not be a popular history book that an undergraduate could possibly publish, but this was something I could work on for years, and maybe eventually contribute my small parcel to the canon of serious Holocaust literature.

Over the next few months I poured my heart into this new research. I was attacking books, and scouring libraries like a PHD candidate with grants and nothing but time and genius at my side. But that wasn't nearly the case. I was still a broke and

---

[6] Data from a recent academic study by a group of researchers at the Holocaust Memorial Museum has shown that under Nazi rule there existed up to 42,500 Nazi ghettos and camps, including brothels, slave labor camps, concentration camps, prisons, hospitals, extermination camps, et al. The research required to catalogue and document such horror has spanned over thirteen years.

perpetually ungraduated college student. I checked out books at local universities that hadn't been checked out since the Dewey Decimal system went digital. I e-mailed relatives of camp survivors and briefly considered learning Romanian.

Over the Christmas break I brought home a ridiculously thick binder with the papers and notes I had compiled to work on until the yuletide arrived. I worked deep into the night while my family slept, and I used more printer ink than I think my father cared for. I was obsessed, despite knowing a future publication of my research was a long shot at best. I continued ordering out-of- print books on Amazon, and reading entire volumes that ended up only mentioning Vapniarka on two or three pages.

Though I could see this project was doomed without more funds and more degrees, I was having a blast, and my love and passion for Holocaust studies grew exponentially over a small period of time. I learned that my future as a famous historian was not likely, but that didn't mean I had to stop my research or my quest for knowledge. For the more I learned about the Holocaust, the more I learned about myself and the vast world that encircled me.

# chapter 7

*"Tragedy is more important than love. Out of all human events, it is tragedy alone that brings people out of their own petty desires and into awareness of other humans' suffering. Tragedy occurs in human lives so that we will learn to reach out and comfort others."*

~C. S. Lewis

I often get asked the following questions when I tell people that I love studying the Holocaust: "Doesn't that depress you?" "Isn't that sad to read about all the time?" "That's kind of morbid isn't it?" The truth is, there are long answers to these simplistic questions, and they are answers that are heavy-laden with philosophy and existentialism. Unfortunately I am not always in the mood to philosophize every time someone asks me about my hobbies.

But I can understand where these people are coming from. The majority of people, even well-educated people, do not always love or know as much about this subject as I do. Anyone with even a minor level of expertise of any sort tends to forget this. So I shouldn't be offended when they ask what seem like ignorant questions. But I am, just a little bit. Telling me it doesn't make sense to study the Holocaust because it elicits depressing thoughts is like saying, "Why do you read your late mother's journals, isn't that deeply saddening?" Of course it's sad, of course it depresses the mind and soul. But is that such a terrible thing, to feel sadness? One would argue that reading a journal of a loved one who had passed away was cathartic and in a way connected them with their past, and though it brought about feelings of remorse and melancholy, it was worth the experience. This is what I believe about the Holocaust. No matter the number of sentences that break my heart and make me weep, it is worth the experience. Though it is not family history, and I am not reading about perished members of my own family, every person or group I read about is part of the human family. And from this family, from this aggregate of humanity, we can find the same connections, the same catharsis and the same sense of joy. A brother to someone else is but a distant brother to me.

The same set of excuses and rationale could be uttered and used about watching the news. Why view a program that just reiterates the evil of mankind, a show that shows us the downward spiraling state of the world? Because it informs us, it teaches us, and it reminds us that there is another side to every story. For every act of hate and oppression you hear about, there are stories of heroism and compassion to be found behind another door. The news is nothing but a present form of history. People are so bored with the facts of yesterday, but so enamored and intrigued by the headlines of today, and what will come tomorrow.

Many a girl has come in and out of my current bedroom. I have a big bed I use as a couch when entertaining guests, and my room is without interruption unlike the communal living room, the common area of four single men in their late twenties. Most girls that enter my room have a similar reaction: "Wow, you have a lot of books" (as if I didn't know I owned many books). It's like telling a very tall person upon meeting them, "Gee, you sure are tall." Well ya, he knows that, and furthermore he has heard that ad nauseam since puberty.

But I understand humans react similarly and habitually, so I don't let it bother me. I just confirm the declaration that my book collection is indeed impressive. After we engage in whatever activities we had planned, i.e. watching movies and making out, the conversation will often (if I have any sway in the matter) return to literature. This is a good sign, usually an indicator that the female in question will be seen again.

Jordan was not a marriage candidate, but she was a lovely girl by every conceivable definition. She found time in the arms of my best friend, and I likewise had swooned over one of her roommates. This bond forced us into the waters of platonic friendship, waters I normally pretend are unswimmable. We flirted and toyed with the idea of intimacy, but we both knew nothing would ever happen. So one night as we lay there, we talked and discussed the contents of my bookshelf. She asked if she could borrow a book and I suggested a few. One I thought she would really enjoy was called *Stolen Innocence*, a book about a young girl that escaped the abuse and dangers of living in a male dominated polygamous sect. Jordan is a mother to a beautiful young daughter, and I thought the story would really resonate with her. Her initial response was a strong and surly, "I can't read that."

So I explained to her that reading hard things was actually a good idea, that it stretched our minds and made us understand people better. I thought to myself, you must feel things, you must experience life. Not reading something because it is grotesque and saddening is akin to not entering a relationship for fear of a broken heart. She retorted by telling me that having a daughter made it too hard to read about things that happened to children (my own mother has told me similar things). She had her reasons, and she wasn't one to be easily cajoled, but I told her that her closeness to her daughter would only make the words and stories that much more relevant and important. She finally acquiesced with a heaping amount of reluctance that she thought she masked well. I was pretty sure she was going to take the book and report back in a couple of weeks that it was too long or that she was too busy to really get into it. But she surprised me and told me about five days later that she had finished the book, and that it "killed her to read, but it was great." She returned it a few days later with a fresh plate of brownies and the admission that I had been right.

So we are brought back to the query. Why do I study the Holocaust? I have never been put behind bars. I have never gone days without food. I have never been bludgeoned or beaten in public. I have never been covered in lice and blood. I have never had loved ones killed. I have never felt a true and crushing sense of hopelessness. So how can I relate? How can I look at the suffering of millions and apply it to my life? How can I learn from an experience I will never endure? The answer is quite simple. All I do to make the Holocaust relevant in my life is alter the scope, and adjust the scale. Sure ,I have never lain in bed at night aching from hunger and disease. But who hasn't been hungry before? Who hasn't felt physical, debilitating pain? Who hasn't known someone that has suffered through or been the victim of a crippling disease?

    Of course I have never been held captive behind barbed wire fences, unable to escape. But I have felt similarly trapped. I have felt like the metaphorical escape into the nearby woods was nothing but a dangerous dream. I have felt like no matter my actions, I would remain in one tragic locale. It's not the same thing. And I am not attempting to compare my plight with that of Holocaust survivors or other victims of extreme tragedy. But when I read about someone's mother being taken away from them in a split second, and the very next moment the father is executed. I relate. I relate because I have a mother, I have a father, and though I haven't experienced such ineffable pain, I can imagine, I can empathize. And the second those words jump from the page to my head, an immense feeling of gratitude hits me. I think about my mother's smell, and my father's embrace. I'm immediately thankful for the safety net they've provided for me my whole life, and I wonder how I would react if they were ruthlessly taken from me. As sentences like these are punctuated I say a silent prayer of thanks that I will never have to lose my parents like that.

    I am well aware that I have not been forced into feeling the extreme hopelessness that the Jewish people felt during the Nazi reign. But I have felt true hopelessness in fleeting moments, moments I don't quickly admit to, in moments when I thought the darkness would never subside. Just because my lack of hope at times is so much smaller and so less intense than that of Holocaust victims, does not and should not minimize my experience. In fact it only enhances that education process for me. Having been through what I only know as hard times, and what to me has felt catastrophic, I feel like I can relate to those who have suffered through unspeakable acts. Everyone has been through things that at the time seemed insurmountable, and unequivocally painful. And reading or learning about others who have been through much more doesn't subtract from our pain, and it does not mitigate our memory. What it does do is connect us. It reminds us that everyone suffers at different times and at very different degrees, but at the end of the day, we all need a little hope, and we could all use a little more compassion.

Now how can you argue that such is not a positive experience? Reading one sentence or one paragraph has the power of imbuing us with gratitude, love, and humility. Is it the power of literature, or the power of the human being, and his story, his struggle, to affect us for the better?

But why does the subject have to be the Holocaust, arguably the darkest chapter in human history? It doesn't have to be. The lessons to be learned and the axiomatic principles are the same with any form of human suffering and tragedy. In the same way I learn about overcoming impossible obstacles to survive by reading a book about Dachau or Auschwitz, I learn by watching a documentary about leukemia or reading an essay on the civil unrest in Darfur. The details are different. The stories are modernized and deal with different groups. But what do we learn? We learn that death is inevitable. We learn that the will to carry on is stronger than we usually imagine. We learn that tragedy can be coupled with joy and triumph.

A few months ago I took to reading the unabridged journals of Sylvia Plath. Though Sylvia is a prodigious poet, and a most beautiful writer, she has some dark stuff—stuff that makes you shiver, stuff that makes you mentally nauseated. And though I have never dealt with suicidal feelings in the least, I have felt the grays and blacks she so vividly puts in verse. But reading about her sadness and her loneliness doesn't make me sink into old feelings of inadequacy or failure, it makes me want to be better. It makes me want to avoid the pitfalls of self-deprecation and depressing thoughts. I salute Sylvia's candidness and willingness to confess with the pen the details of her tortured soul. Though I wouldn't suggest this book to someone who was clinically depressed or questioning whether life was worth living, it is a work that has motivated me. I see how bipolar her feelings were and how the will to fight and move on was there at times, but effervesced at the end of her young life. It is another written reminder that things can seem hopeless, but there is a way out.

In the same manner that I read this painful autobiographical account, I read testimonies of Holocaust survivors. In a book called *Holocaust Testimonies: The Ruins of Memory,* a Holocaust survivor known simply as Philip K. gives his account of life after the camps:

> I often say to people who pretend or seem to be marveling at the fact that I seem to be so normal, so unperturbed and so capable of functioning—they seem to think the Holocaust passed over and it's done with: it's my skin. This is not a coat. You can't take it off. And it's there, and it will be there until I die....

After my eyes take in a powerful quote like this I am not emotionally crushed, but rather I want to understand that person better. I will likely not come into contact with too many Holocaust survivors as the years pass by, but I will undoubtedly meet people with their own layers of memory that have become more than a removable article of clothing, but a part of their body, a part of their everyday forever, their skin. So, in understanding one person's grief and life of sadness, I am better able to love and understand others with similar or completely different scars from yesterday. Some scars will be fresh and painful reminders, others will be but painful memories visible on the surface.

Even having lived a life fairly bereft of tragedy, I know that I possess both removable coats and permanent skin, things that are often with me, but that won't last, and things that are fused into my physical being, things I cannot rid myself of. And I am at peace with this realization. There are so many events and moments in your life that stay with you for better or for worse; it is not a matter of being unaffected. It is about accepting the effects, and making them steer you towards a greater, more elevated place.

Another reason I find it eternally imperative to study the sad stories and heart-crushing accounts of human folly is because it teaches us certain lessons that we are unlikely to learn on the same level elsewhere. The lessons I am referring to are the ones that teach us how to overcome, how to fight when we have no fight left, and how to move on when we feel ten feet deep in drying concrete. When we read about individuals that escaped from the darkest prisons in history and lived to tell about it, how can we feel hopeless about the things that hold us captive? Maybe the odious night-watcher, the sadistic prison guard for you is nicotine. Perhaps you have tried to run away before, only to be dragged back in. Or is it possible that you have not tried to run away because it seems utterly useless, for nicotine will surely track you down and imprison you again?

Maybe cigarettes, nary a single toxic chemical on this planet have the power to incarcerate you. What about pornography, or similarly insidious addictions of the libido? Surely one addicted to inappropriate and lewd urges must feel a sense of incarceration and captivity. Whatever the vice, no matter the gravity of struggle, and depth of the hole you've dug for yourself, it cannot be worse than that thing that millions before you have not only suffered but beaten, and triumphed. In the case of studying persons of the Holocaust we can come face to face with the stark reality: many did not escape the camps, and in fact the overwhelming majority perished at the hands of their captors. But there were victors, there were handfuls and pockets of people that were not just going to accept defeat, were not going to let someone else decide their fate.

These people lived and have enriched the world with their harrowing stories of beating unbeatable odds, leaving us with testimonies of the impossible.

Does that mean trying your hardest and having a determined and unbreakable spirit will ensure success, triumph and happiness? It will not. Life does not handout indelible certificates ensuring your place among the happy, healthy, and living. There simply exist no guarantees, other than the inevitable wind of change. But in reading and hearing about such monumental victories, such faith-inspiring stories of overcoming, stories of freedom, I am reminded of the principle of hope. I am reminded that impossible is not four unbreakable walls; impossible is an evil invention, an imaginary force that tells us we cannot and should not. It's nothing but a devilish figment.

Most days a voice, whether self-contrived or otherwise influenced, whispers to me that one thing or another is impossible. Unfortunately I tend to believe this mendacious uttering. I know I can do better, I know I can achieve more than I am achieving, but the voice persists, and convinces me daily that what I want to do will not be done, and what I ultimately desire is not really in reach. At the end of the day, I know the whispers are not true. I know I can do great things, and accomplish things I have not even imagined yet, but it is easier to listen to the notion of impossibility. And easier usually wins in battles of the self.

In frequently immersing myself in literature of the Holocaust and other world tragedies I am reminded of all these things: that impossible is nothing, that hope is fleeting but real and necessary, that walls that reach the clouds can be climbed, and lakes that stretch across continents can be traversed. You could compare it to someone who reads a little quote book every day. A little inspiration in the form of letters can change the course of a day, and one changed day can change an entire life. But for me, I need more than to just read a few sentences or watch a few minutes of an inspirational YouTube video. I need writings and words to not just hit my brain, but enter my soul like bees rushing into their waiting hive.

So I read, and I read voraciously. I try to understand the lives of others through the words that they have left behind, in hopes that I will be a better man for it.

# chapter 8

*"Often the strongest blades were pounded the hardest, or scorched the most severely; we judge them by their strength and sharpness, not by their prior rough experiences. With our comrades it should be the same. A good blade is rarely forged in a velvet box."*

~Orsov

The percentage of people that have survived something so awesomely terrible as the Holocaust, the Gulags, the killings in Rwanda, or any other genocidal evil is so minuscule in comparison to the sea of humanity that has crashed into the shore of human existence. The average person has not been the victim of tyranny or the subject of some hateful human torture. But this in no way means we are without trials, without immense and soul-squashing struggles. Though my life has been relatively without thorns, the thorns that have pricked me along the way have left me bloody and full of tears just like someone who has had a life with nothing but briars and thorns lining the ground, an unavoidable path coupled with unshod feet and a labyrinthine road to relief.

My own trials are deep-rooted and trivial, haunting, and forgettable. I have done hard things, and I have quit when things got tough. I have overcome what I thought would never be beaten, and I have succumbed to my own weaknesses and failed. I think this is more or less the experience of every human to some degree. We all kind of teeter-totter through life knowing every type of emotion and every shape of defeat, glory, and sadness, whether we realize it or not. My own story that is very much unfinished will not elicit much sympathy, nonetheless it is my journey, and my trials and adversities, my enemies and my friends, have all made up what my life currently is, and hopefully what it can become.

When I was nineteen I moved to Rio de Janeiro for two years of my life. I wanted to proselyte. I was young, but I had strong Christian beliefs and wanted to share them with the world. I didn't know Portuguese, and I had no idea what the next twenty-four months would entail. I knew I didn't love beans, and that I had a sensitive stomach, but I didn't realize beans and various porcine parts would be a consistent part of every lunch for the next 700-odd days. I didn't think I would be hospitalized for an "augmented spleen" or that I would have my entire big toenail removed without anesthesia. And I had no idea how difficult it would be to become fluent in another language in such a short period of time.

I adored my time in Brazil. It was unforgettable and absolutely changed the trajectory of my life. And I hope I made some small impact on those I taught and befriended. But uprooting my life in America to live in one of the most dangerous cities in the world was anything but breezy. Early on in my ministry while I was still grappling with the foreign tongue and the absurd humidity I read a verse in the Bible that seemed to speak quietly in my ear every remaining day I had in that hot beautiful country. Paul famously states in the second book of Corinthians that, "… I take pleasure in infirmities, in reproaches, in necessities, in persecutions, in distresses for Christ's sake: for when I am weak, then am I strong." The final words were underscored in my brain, 'when I am weak, I am strong.' It was such a simple notion, and applicable in every aspect of life. Sure, I was attempting the work of Christ. But my distresses, reproaches, and tribulations, no matter for whose sake, could equate to strength, and despite its obvious message, it was new and splendid revelation for a woefully inexperienced nineteen year old. It is interesting to me how certain words or verses heard a thousand times before can suddenly and intensely resonate with you. That's what happened to me, and the rest of my time in the slums, running away from rabid dogs and being far too close to gunfire, was done with joy and the knowledge that no matter how I stumbled or saw my weaknesses magnified, all the while I was being fortified.

This life lesson I learned from a simple scripture has stayed with me over the years and has reminded me that my tears don't have to be in vain, and that my poor decisions and failures can be all for some greater purpose.

Being a bachelor in my late twenties, the bulk of my sorrows go into a torn cardboard box labeled "Broken Heart." This doesn't just mean rejection or unrequited love. Yes, I have been dumped and unloved my share of times, but there is much more that can break a heart. Moving away from all my friends at age fourteen broke my heart. Seeing my Dad writhe in pain from chronic back pain has broken my heart. Seeing my Mom cry has broken my heart more than one time. Looking back at the last time I held my grandpa's swollen hand in a hospital bed before he passed, that broke my heart.

And though there is plenty to sadden a weary heart that has been broken time and time again, I find endless hope and joy around me. And I manage to do this while I read book after book about the Holocaust, arguably the most tragic scene in the history of the earth. How can this be? How can I look at gray clouds all day and see a golden sun? I guess it is my knowledge that the clouds will pass. Sometimes it will rain first, but they will pass and bring rays of light that remind us that it will be okay.

I can't seem to see my life as being off-kilter and screwed up when I am entrenched in the literature of Auschwitz, or reading the tales of Buchenwald or Treblinka. No matter my day, or the weight and size of the cross I am carrying, my twenty-four hour day is paradise compared to those killing centers. And when I read about victims that found solace in reciting poetry, found beauty in the birds, and kindness by the hands of a stranger, I know I can find beauty, poetry, joy and anything magnificent that I want in my own life. Oscar Wilde said, "With freedom, books, flowers, and the moon, who could not be happy?"

Some people find it morose to poeticize or romanticize such a dark thing. They find it unwholesome and disturbing to look again and again at death, at loss, and at terror. But why not learn from these things, and find beauty in the cracks of the rotting wood, rather than casting it into the fire? What good does it do to forget history, or look at it once and then sweep it beneath the floorboards? If examined properly, history should echo in our minds for the rest of our lives, giving us a greater understanding of the world and of men.

There is however a therapeutic caveat, one we have all heard 27,000 times: it is easier said than done. It is easy to say, "Don't be depressed, people all over the world have it much worse." Or my favorite, "Chin up, it could be worse." Of course it could be worse. Even the dimmest of individuals are cognizant that things could be worse. You may have cancer, but at least you aren't blind. Or you may have just lost a loved one, but at least *you* have your health. All of these consolation thoughts are not super helpful, especially in moments of agony. And that is because there is no novelty to their ideas. But the point of reading and understanding people and cultures better is to enable a sort of storage system in your brain where you can put motivational words and encouraging adages in the hopes of finding them when you need them, dusting them off, and using them to make your own life richer. Putting these uplifting stories and smile-inducing anecdotes in the storage unit does not, however, ensure that they will be quickly found with ease when you need them. You have to want to find them, and be willing to look for them when the shed is dark and you can't summon the strength to turn on the light.

No one is immune to the evils of being bummed out. It doesn't matter how much uplifting literature you read, or how many paradigm-altering TED Talks you watch. The blues will come. But if you have not stored your garage with the occasional tale of heroism, or a box full of uplifting words, it will be harder to summon that feeling of happy when the days are dreary, long, and without hope.

I try to awaken all of my senses to fight off the tide of melancholy. For me, I must have human contact; I have to listen to musical lyrics that remind me that others have been through what I have been through. I have to watch films and documentaries about life and the struggle of getting past barriers. I have to read omnivorously to better understand the worlds people live in, and the things that all humans think, but few articulate. Maybe I am emotionally needy. I cannot neglect any of the emotional sectors in my brain or feelings of loneliness and discouragement, or anger will arise. Some people were blessed with quite the unique ability to be unshaken by the tremors of life. But I am convinced these people are innate humanitarians, the kind of people that seek to better understand the world and the people they come in contact with. And maybe they don't read dozens of books about prisoners of war and victims of pernicious regimes, but I doubt they would shy away from learning about them, and gleaning every ounce of light from the darkness of the past.

# chapter 9

> *"People can get so easily disturbed by social, general, and universal evil that they ignore the evil inside themselves."*
>
> ~Bishop Auxentios

When you visit a place like Auschwitz, you come to realize what true evil looks like. Though I only understood an absurdly small fraction of what those unlucky souls who actually passed through the gates as prisoners went through, evil nonetheless accosted me. Just like reading a book about the 9/11 Terrorist Attacks will only give you a glimpse into the tiniest portion of the kaleidoscope of evil you will feel in contrast with actually visiting Ground Zero, or talking with someone that was in the collapsing Twin Towers, reading the book is still an important act. But for me, walking the dusty roads and crumbling corridors of the camp seemed to awaken the beast that I always knew existed. But I had never heard him breath, I had never smelled his putrid breath or seen his awful blood-soaked claws. I simply was aware of his residence.

You can read libraries of theses and caves of historic works, but until you see the scratches on the wall, and see the machinery that murdered millions, the beast known as evil is but an abstract thing, a dormant force. But having that malicious creature awoken and upright I started to think about more than just the Holocaust and its perpetrators, more than just the ethnic cleansing in Albania, the suicide bombers in Pakistan, or the drug related homicides in Columbia. I started to think about the evil inside myself, and what I was capable of. Of course this portion of evil, this tiny beast sleeping somewhere inside me, was not capable of mass murder or true crimes against humanity. I know myself. I am a decent guy. But it made me wonder about that beast, and what I was capable of. I am sure no Nazi or serial killer at a young age would say, "Ya, I will ruthlessly take life. I will obliterate generations." People aren't born this way, they don't take their first breath of air and become evil. It insidiously creeps up on them in one form or another for a million different reasons. The beast will flash his teeth and growl that terrible growl, but it is up to every individual whether he or she will be dominated by this animal.

    Peering into my own soul and my own desires I started to think about the bad things I have done, the evil that I have participated in. Of course it is all relative. What I consider to be untoward and inappropriate may appear innocuous and acceptable to others. But the truth is there are certain sins whether of commission or omission that will never be okay, they will never perpetuate good or pull the human race forward. So wherein lies our excuse?

    So I asked myself, what is it that I consistently or often do that is pulling the world down, even by immeasurable proportions? I know I am not doing anything egregious. Sometimes I use foul language. Sometimes I don't really listen to people that are earnestly trying to tell me something. Other times I carelessly tell a half truth. But surely there are still other things I do that only add oil to the lamp of evil. And though a few drops here and there or maybe even a dozen gallons of accumulated oil over the years will not compare to the evil that floods the earth, I am not okay with adding to it. For it only takes one drop of oil to start a fire. And the flames in their bright orange destruction can cause irreparable damage and loss, whether we see the ruinous outcome or not.

Although I live a life of annotation, filling up journals, buying sticky notes on a monthly basis, underscoring and highlighting my books, and filling the internet with my opinions and words, I find that like most people, I withhold truth. Even in my journals, which are prolix and raw, I leave out ugly details of unrighteous thoughts and unkind deeds. Maybe I want my progeny to think I was a better man. Maybe seeing the words of misdeed in print are too much for my hubris.

But I don't think I am alone in this. Who has not lied to a friend? Who has not said hurtful things to a brother? Who has not made their mother cry? Who has not recklessly broken a heart? Now of course you can argue that we all make mistakes, that we are human. And this is a reasonable argument, for a life without error is impossible and probably lacking in any real purpose. But small evils add up, not in a numerical way that will eventually equate to some punitive consequence, but when one becomes two and two becomes twenty, these things can become habit. And when doing a small evil becomes habitual, it opens the door for greater evils to sneak in and lay wait under our beds, procuring the chance to grab our feet and pull us down when we get out of bed. And just like we don't usually check under our beds for monsters, we don't usually self-evaluate. We do sometimes, but is it with full truth and complete openness to change and ameliorate ourselves? This is a rare and beautiful practice that if turned habitual could affect the world for the better. None of us are perfect, but our responsibility as human beings is to mitigate our mistakes, and try to be better tomorrow, and in doing so we are eliminating some portion of evil from the earth, some corner of a snowflake that flurries about in the blizzard of evil. We might not be killing the beast, but we can shut him up; we can bind him and revoke his powers.

A couple of years ago I did something terrible. When this thing started I did not even consider it wrong. But as certain things transpired I came to realize I had done something rather menacing and hurtful.

Let's give some background first. One of my best friends Marc and I have had somewhat of a running conversation for years on Facebook. He lives an hour away from me and is married with a young daughter. I don't see him as much as I like, but I have known him for fourteen plus years. We talk on almost a daily basis, even if it is just to remind the other of a new song to listen to, or a simple "Love you bud, night." Sometimes one of us won't respond for a few days, but the conversation picks up where it left off and continues on into the eternities, or so it seems. Our talks are trivial, stupid, and sometimes deep as you could imagine. We delve into taboo subjects, and discuss our friends. We encourage each other, remind each other of our goals, and make fun of the people we love. It is a beautiful back and forth, a correspondence made easy and wonderful in our digital age. In another time we would have sent long and thought-out letters, but we are blessed with an age of ease. So it goes, day after day, year after year we talk, catch up, reminisce, and vent.

    We have another best friend Paxton, an essential part of a circle of friends whose bond knows no bounds. He lives but a few miles from me, and has lived with me several times over the past six years. He is tall and painfully handsome. He walks around like the ground is made of diamonds and the clouds are full of nectar. For better or worse he is under the impression that every human he comes in contact with is a fantastic person. We also have been friends for fourteen plus years, and speak nearly every day. We have a strange habit of kissing each other on the shoulder when we embrace. We do this mostly because it amuses us and it often goes unseen. When it is witnessed it usually just elicits a few looks of bewilderment, or people assume they didn't see what they thought they saw. It is a byproduct of a strong and strange friendship, for I think that any strong friendship is a little strange if examined closely.

Paxton and I have been eternal bachelors swimming in the same dating pool together for quite some time, while the more reasonable and generally responsible Marc was wed nearly five years ago. We have waded through unfruitful double dates, broken hearts, and jaded feelings. But suddenly and without any real warning Paxton found his match. They courted in a fiercely quick manner before deciding to get engaged. Only weeks after discovering that my boy had entered an exclusive relationship for the first time in years did I find out there was a wedding happening in just a couple months. The truth is, I was a little bummed. I had lost dozens of friends to their wives, but one of my final wingmen was now slipping away. But I was happy for him. My eternally happy friend was even happier than usual, and full of an excitement I had never seen in him. His speech was different, and I knew he would figure it out even though I felt the matrimony was rushed.

They were soon married, and I was the best man. I toasted to their future with perfect comedic timing and warmth. As the months rolled on I didn't see much of them. I saw frequent photos posted online, and had the occasional lunch with my buddy. But things had changed, and maybe that is just how it goes. The future is never quite what you thought it would be, and sometimes that is okay.

Marc and I started discussing their marriage at great length online. We talked about his wife, about her family, and about their prudish love life. I didn't realize it, but we sometimes talked about our friend Paxton and his choices and decisions for hours at a time. Mostly it was playful jest mixed with critical judgement, the kind only friends can give to each other. But we weren't expressing our concerns or doubts about their marriage to Paxton. We were just enjoying our time in our splendid ivory tower.

I knew we were being a bit gossipy and maybe a little harsh with our words, but who cared, it was just secret banter between two friends, idle chatter incapable of injurious outcomes. In the midst of our ongoing assessment of our best friend's future I had forgotten two very important things. Firstly, that Paxton was a very curious person. Secondly, that at some point months ago I had given him my Facebook password for some forgettable reason. I never suspected that he would open up my messages, let alone take the time to read through the pages and pages of dross that Marc and I had written about. But he did. He did, and it hurt him, it gouged at his sensitivity, and it opened up wounds that were probably already around, but still, that hurts. I also didn't suspect that upon reading the rubbish we had composed, that he would share it with his new bride.

The timetable of these events gets a little murky for me. I don't know how long Paxton sat on this information before he sent me a heated text of accusation, disappointment, and confession. But it's irrelevant. Paxton was very upset, and though he was not in the right by snooping through pages and pages of dialogue that was supposed to be behind an implicitly locked door, he kind of had every right to feel deeply bothered and betrayed.

Being friends on what I considered to be a metaphysical level, I knew this incident was not going to end anything. I knew it would be unpleasant and full of unwanted tension, but true friends are always friends. The inevitable confrontation ensued and we both, along with Marc, felt an untoward remorse; we were both in the wrong, and somehow had let an evil inside us peek its head out. There it was taunting us and telling us we were bad people, as evil desires nothing more than to rid us of our peace and our hope. After some hard words we both came to a place that killed the evil, a place where any semblance of iniquity will be smothered and asphyxiated: forgiveness. We forgave each other and decided to move on. I apologized profusely, and wrote his wife a letter in an attempt to make amends and move forward, and so did Marc. As Jean Genet said: "To write is your last resort when you have betrayed someone."

Sadly, she never responded or even acknowledged our apologies. About a month later with no warning, Paxton's wife left him. He came home from work one day and all of her things were gone. She was gone. Love was gone. I came over and slept in his bed with him that night. I have never seen him like that. And again we were friends, best friends.

To this day I am still bothered by my actions. How could I do that? How could I be so callous, so obtuse? That is the nature of the evil within us. We think we have a firm grasp on what we are capable of, and what we would or wouldn't do in a given situation. But who is to say? Would I join the Nazi party if I was conditioned to believe in their dogma by decades of influence? I like to think I wouldn't. But what if my parents were staunch anti-Semites? What if my school teachers taught me at a young age that Jews were vermin? What if the pervading laws in my country dictated that Jews were subhuman and had to be marked by a Davidic star on their clothing? I still like to think I would rise above, floating on to a higher echelon of understanding, love, and sophistication. But what if I was a political man, swayed by the very words of Hitler himself? Would I participate in the horrors of a concentration camp? I cannot think of anything more abhorrent. But how do I know for sure what I would do in a hypothetical situation that never has and never will arise?

I think of the vilest humans in history, men that escorted women and children to their deaths with malicious smiles and haughty demeanors. I could never act in that way. But what am I doing when I openly make fun of someone, with a smug grin? Am I not momentarily killing their soul? Am I not escorting them to a place of sadness? Of course this is a stretch, an absurd scale mitigation, but it is true. The Holocaust is a microcosm of life, of the world we live in and the ubiquity of evil, of mistakes, of moving on, and of witnessing darkness.

No one plans on growing up to neglect their kids. No one hopes for a future addicted to drugs. No child envisions a life of violence and hate, yet this and many other unplanned futures come to sad fruition. Why? Because evil is not something we are born with. It is not something that we either have within us or don't. It is something far more complicated, a force much more stealthy and insidious than we realize at first glance. Evil thrives off of hopelessness; it lives off of backing people into corners. No one assumes that one day they will rob a convenience store, but that same person probably never thought they would be on welfare, without enough money to feed their crying children. The desperation at hand can beget the evil you never thought you were capable of.

Does this mean we are under some sort of twisted obligation to forgive and understand the deeds of Holocaust perpetrators? Does this mean we are to sympathize with serial killers, and rationalize riotous acts? No. This idea, this notion that evil is something that creeps up on us, is not an excuse. It is a reminder, a warning, a life-saving, life-hanging caveat.

For me personally, it is a reminder to adjust my life when I see evil encroaching. It usually comes in small, subtle ways. I find myself gossiping. I find myself tearing down someone. I find myself viewing the world through the most narrowing and confining ocular apparatus. For evil does not encourage anything past oneself. Evil is selfishness and vanity magnified and personified. So, I find myself forgetting or neglecting those who are always there for me, those who deserve more attention, more love. You could easily argue that this type of thing is not evil, simply the nature of human folly. But I would opine that for the majority of humans abstaining from evil, eliminating malice from one's life, is not so much a matter of commission, but of omission. Most of us will never come face to face with the likes of an Auschwitz. Most of us will never have enough power or influence to generate such evil. But many, if not most of us, will find ourselves in a similar position as that of the many German citizens. Many German, Polish, Hungarian, or other national citizens, overtaken by the iron fist of Nazism or Stalinism, could have done more, could have asked more questions, and likely could have saved a few lives. After all, the concentration camps would have been impossible without the cooperation of railway stations, acquiescing governments, and quiet, silenced citizens. As Primo Levi points out, "Monsters exist, but they are too few in number to be truly dangerous. More dangerous are the common men, the functionaries ready to believe and to act without asking questions." Not to say things could have been overthrown or avoided, but the scope of things could have certainly been reduced in some small percentage had certain individuals and groups made a decision to do something.

    With that thread of thought I think I know where my real evil rests its ugly head. For me it isn't in violence, vanity, or abuse; it is in not doing more good. I consider myself a rather kind and considerate person. I don't hold grudges. I am usually loving, and could sometimes even be described as generous. But I am well aware that my niceness, my love, my honesty is sometimes dependent on how I feel, or what I feel others deserve. In having no apparent cache of hateful feelings or malevolent plans I like to think my potential for goodness, for love, is great. And I cannot think of a greater sin I could commit than to fall short of my potential to influence the world for better. I hate to think of the very real possibility that there are many people that at the end of my life I could have helped, but simply chose not to. I cringe thinking about people I could have loved more, people I could have made smile or dance with joy, but because I was too caught up in my own life, too jaded, or simply too lazy, I did not. It pains me to think of the last days of my life as days of regret, not because I never hiked Kilimanjaro, or because I never made a million dollars, but because I did not do as much good as I could have: maybe just an unsent text, an unmailed letter, a forgotten hug, a neglected kiss. To me, that regret, that pain, that fear, would be a consequence of my own evil that lived deep within my troubled soul.

I read a single sentence some time ago that will not leave my blood. It is in there like a floating tattoo, reminding me of a most simplistic principle. It was uttered by a survivor of the dark, a victor of death and hate, Viktor Frankel, a quintessential author of the Holocaust, also a highly respected and published psychologist. He said in no uncertain verbiage: "No one has the right to do wrong, not even when wrong has been done to them." Of course this sentiment has been echoed and repeated by great men and women from Moses and Mother Teresa to Martin Luther King. But Frankel's words seem to make it more definitive. His statement has no political or religious backing; it merely enforces a philosophy of humanness, a principle of basic human goodness.

As most axiomatic phrases go, they are easier written, easier spoken, than practiced. But if I am going to take philosophical advice concerning goodwill, right, and wrong, it is going to be from a man who survived unthinkable horrors, and only a few years after wrote about finding light in the darkness, who did not retaliate or succumb to the level of those who mistreated him. Perhaps we will never reach such an enlightened viewpoint, one whereupon hearing poisonous words about ourselves, we don't instinctively strike back. Maybe we won't ever fully heed to this wise creed, but what an awesome goal. That is why it is in my veins. Not because I adhere to its doctrine perfectly, but because I need the reminder. I need the ideology of it stamped into my body and brain so that I may more fully reach my potential, so that I may be a better, more refined version of myself, a version capable of so much more.

# chapter 10

*"God will not look you over for medals, degrees or diplomas but for scars."*

~Elbert Hubbard

I embark on this chapter with awkward trepidation. I don't want to write it. I don't want to confront it. But I would be doing a disservice to myself if I skipped the issue, acting like it had no relevance in my own life or the lives of others. And truth be told, what I consider a vital issue to discuss could very well be moot to many people. In fact, it might be for my own catharsis, as most writing tends to be more personal and vain than it is advertised. So whether this chapter is for you, or for me, or both of us, it must be written.

Going to Auschwitz, and being there as a visitor of foreign soils, hoping to learn, hoping to gain access to an unthinkable portal—all of this is eternally different from being incarcerated there, being there not for knowledge's sake, but by sheer and cruel obligation.

However, both parties, both individuals, come face to face with God. Maybe you come face to face with your own bitter atheism, or a frustrated and violent form of nihilism. Perhaps you feel a closer connection with the great Jehovah. Whether it's an approximation to deity, a divorcing of beliefs, an apathy for faith, or a zest for higher power, no matter your past convictions, or your present state of religiousness, entering the Holocaust via a boxcar, a tour bus, a documentary, or an old book, you are forced to ask yourself questions, to wonder, and to ponder with pain. You have to stop and ask yourself if what you've always believed in and trusted is true.

The studying of the Holocaust or participation thereof can be the most existentially troubling or awakening of subjects. To remain unprovoked, unstirred intellectually, spiritually, and physically is to ignore the past, a conscious refusal to cope with and feel what is undoubtedly enveloping your every sense.

For me, a Christian, a man with firm and rooted beliefs, walking through the gates of Auschwitz, seeing bricks that formed the Warsaw Ghetto, visiting Jewish museums, reading survivor accounts, all touched me in a profound way. I can't speak for those who have never believed in a supreme being, or for those who have lost what faith they used to cling to. But I know what I feel. And feelings are just as empirical to me as written documents and archived facts.

When I first arrived in that corner of Europe that brought about so much pain and death, I felt the presence of God. It is easy to refute my feelings since I neither endured nor know anyone personally that endured the grimy claws of the Holocaust. But I don't need to justify my feelings. I felt the same peace and solemnity there that I felt walking through grass and white tombstones in the twilight at Gettysburg. You can say, "Well of course you felt 'peace,' it's quiet and everyone around is trying to be respectful, and ya, death makes people contemplate their own mortality, ergo, peace." But it is not that simply answered to me. I felt more than just a calm, but I felt a presence. I'm not saying I had a vision or some ephemeral out of body experience, I am just saying I felt an unmistakable comfort in what could be considered an uncomfortable place.

Before I walked into Auschwitz I prayed. I prayed for a better understanding, but I didn't ask God for absolute answers because I knew there were none that would satiate my distressed curiosities. Even as I prayed, I wondered with great worry if my prayers were enough.

Months after my trip to Auschwitz I awoke in the dark of the night with a terrifying and vivid thought. The next morning I scribbled furiously what I could remember. I scratched down the following words in a small black notebook:

> A certain thought woke me up. I imagined at the end of my life a sort of demonstration of all the prayers I had given, a physical scroll unraveled, revealing every word I ever uttered to my Creator. I saw before me the scrolls of other people. Some seemed to stretch on forever in tiny print, while others had but a few lines. I wondered whose would be most interesting to read. Then I wondered if mine would elicit any real intrigue.

> Were mine beautiful words sent heavenward in both times of defeat and triumph? Or were they lifeless repetitions haphazardly hurled above me with wavering consistency? My scroll was hidden, for my heart still held a beat. But I feared for the latter. I feared that when I met my Maker my scroll would be inadequate for Him that saved me.

I won't dive head first into my religious beliefs, but I will openly talk about faith. Faith is something difficult to describe, difficult to have, yet so vital for millions if not billions of people on this earth. For me faith is equated with reason and sense. Without faith very little makes sense, and I imagine my life would feel rudderless and bereft of meaning if I had no faith whatsoever. Faith reminds me that there is purpose in things, even in terrible chaos and tremendous sadness. It does not mean I understand the purpose or even like the purposes; alas it is but a small voice telling me it will be alright and that all will make sense one day, be it in this life or the next.

This acquisition of faith in no way means that one understands and is at peace with the Holocaust and its aftermath, or any tragedy or horror for that matter. It just provides a little peace in the heart, a drip of solace where one's natural reaction is to feel bitterness, confusion, and hate. Faith rather chips away at the blackness that takes over the heart as terrible things start to happen.

Many would argue that my faith or the faith of others is blind. How could one believe in such a benevolent force that would permit such heinous things to happen? But do people not have similar "blind" faith in the sciences? We all accept laws of physics and cosmology whether we understand them or not. I don't understand how gravity and magnetic energies work. And it doesn't make sense to me why the earth does certain things. But I believe. I understand that a world without unanswered questions does not and will never exist.

Once again, maybe it is easy for a person of my background to have faith. Brought up Christian, with few tragedies and but a plebeian modicum of struggle. But how would a survivor of the Holocaust keep their faith? How could someone that has seen evil in its purest form believe in good? How could a person who had experienced years of unanswered prayers believe in someone or something being on the other end of their prayers? There is no way to know how our faith might waver or disintegrate if we had to lose a brother to the flames, or if we saw infants thrown into a massive fire. How could it not change our belief system? Truth is, many survivors of the Holocaust that had been faithful practitioners of the Jewish religion their whole lives lost their faith. We say lost, but in many instances that faith was not lost but buried, buried deep somewhere so distant and subterranean that it could never be retrieved or rekindled. And who could blame one for abandoning their faith after such an ordeal?

Writer Teddy Weinberger wrote down a small piece in 2009 recollecting a conversation he had with two Holocaust survivors that he was close to. They discussed God, religion, and as Teddy said, "The big questions." The answers that these two elderly survivors gave are varied, expectant and surprising. Near the end of their lives together, Harry and Llona Rosenberg recalled some of the feelings they had, and some of their emotions and beliefs that remained. Both of them saw the unspeakable and endured the unthinkable, but their attitudes over a half century later are the revealing clue to this ontological puzzle.

In reaction to the initial horror of the Holocaust, Harry spoke rather definitively: "If God does this, then I don't believe in God." Weinberger goes on to tell how after the war Harry's belief in God returned. As straightforward and tersely as before the war, Harry sings a different tune: "I don't have any complaints against the Master of the Universe, it's the people you have to watch out for. After the war, anger would have tied me to the past at a time when I desperately needed to start thinking about my present and my future life. In the next life, I don't expect any answers from God, but I do have some questions for him."

Harry's words are beautiful and typical of the vacillating nature of human beings. Both of his positions on God feel merited and justifiable. I have never worn the broken shoes nary have I walked through the blood-soaked mud of an actual hell. But I know life throws things at us, leaving our faith as precarious as a leaf in autumn. We speak in absolutes, but our universe changes and our absolutes break and take new forms.

Llona similarly displayed a range of beliefs perhaps atypical of one who has undergone such godless tragedy. Though I don't know to what degree Llona suffered, nor do I know the specificity of the terror she witnessed, her faith proved immutable as she said, "There was never a point when I stopped believing in God." Harry and Llona went on to explain how they continued in a path of religious pursuit after the war. Their words didn't reveal a perfect knowledge or acceptance of things, but rather a hope, a faith that indeed there was a reason for the suffering, and a place of deserving rest for the countless martyrs who died before them. Harry ended the interview with some touching words of hope, "I really hope there is a Gan Eden[7], because Gehenum[8] I saw already in my life."

I know every blessed and beautiful soul on this earth has felt portions of heaven, and terrible glimpses into 'Gehenum.' Going through one can remind you of the existence of the other, which I think is a good thing. It is good to know that bliss fades, and pain will subside. Life will get tangled and unfathomably messy, but it will also turn on a dime and show you how happy you can be. Recognizing hell as a part of life will only help us live a life without panic, depression, and despair.

An encapsulating summation to this idea of theodicy[9] is explained beautifully by Rabbi Alan Lurie in his article, *"How Could God Have Allowed the Holocaust?"*

---

[7] The Hebrew word Gan is literally translated as Garden. The word Gan can also stand alone to mean Garden of Eden.

[8] Also written Gehenna, Gehinnom, or Gehinnam—refers to the ancient valley of the Son of Hinnom in Jerusalem. Due to Jewish religious tradition and cultural use, Gehenna became a metonym for "Hell," or any similar place of torture and punishment in the afterlife.

[9] A vindication of the divine attributes, particularly holiness and justice, in establishing or allowing the existence of physical and moral evil.

Where was God in the Holocaust? As God knew the terrible choices made by too many, and wept at the horrific consequences, those who chose love and service in the face of this horror were strengthened and consoled. Good eventually did win over evil, by our own hands.

We can be mad at God for the Holocaust or for other human tragedies, but this is like a teenager who begs you to let him drive a car —promising to be responsible— gets drunk, crashes in to a telephone pole, and then blames you for giving him the keys. If we agree that humanity must have free will, we must accept the consequences of its decisions. As Elie Wiesel wrote: "After the Holocaust I did not lose faith in God. I lost faith in mankind.

# chapter 11

*"In many ways, history both begins and ends with questions; which is to say that it never really ends, but is a process."*

~John H. Arnold

History and life are two connected realities. They both change every day based on new events and recent discoveries. They both cause pain, and they teach, remind, and influence us. They both will give us definitive answers, and they both can leave us directionless and more confused than when we started. They are both beautiful and awful. But ultimately, they are both an experience, more of a process than a single unchanging event in time.

Certain life experiences or events in history will undoubtedly leave us much more conflicted than others. The Holocaust is one of those things. It seems to elicit more questions the deeper down you dig. You can study the ins and outs of the Nazi regime, and you may understand more clearly how the hate against the Jews was orchestrated, but an unstoppable wave of questions will crash into your mind: internal questions, hard questions. The more historical facts you obtain, the less you will seem to understand the whys and hows, no matter how many thesis papers and volumes you read on those very whys and hows.

It really is a great paradox. As I walked past the entrance of Auschwitz, a sinister jaunt that millions of victims and tourists alike have taken before me, I was given answers no amount of turned pages could reveal to me. But at the same time I was flushed with even more questions than I ever realized I had. Again I thought about the feet that preceded mine. How much snow gathered in that specific path on winter days? How much smoke was visible to the prisoners, amidst the many trees and brick buildings? What about on a windy, overcast day? What would the ground look like at night, or during a storm? Thoughts that never entered my studious mind entered and multiplied like rabbits. What did the Nazi guards smell like? Did they reek of alcohol and gun powder? Was the evil something you could almost notice with your nose? I wondered about sounds. I wondered about aerial views of the camp. I wondered about the earth that lay silently beneath the wasteland ever so aware of the terror above, but silenced by thick levels of dirt and rock. I started wondering about the intricacies of the SS uniforms, and the lice infested prison garb. My mind could not keep up with the scenery or with the truth of things.

I had seen pictures of the gas chambers. They are usually black and white, and pretty stark. They hit you with a punch of reality, a reality that also seems a little surreal, like reading about the dinosaurs. But as I walked into the chambers with my own feet, and touched the walls and ovens with my own fingers, untold amounts of questions arose. I knew they would never be answered in full, and that added to my sadness, and to the realness of my experience. It was so emotionally confusing, because the answers I received there, historical facts, and geographical explanations at first satiated me, then quickly jettisoned me into a pool of whirling questions, ever multiplying, and ever more excruciating.

For a few minutes after I walked out of those dimly lit corridors that were damp and haunting, I felt that sad feeling of confusion, that feeling that any answers I got from walking in only turned into a thousand more questions as I walked out. But after some thought, I realized this was not such a terrible thing.

So much of life is wasted in pondering the troublesome state we seem to find ourselves in. There are thousands of things to worry about, and a circular infinity of questions that cannot all be answered. But I think the joy of the journey is in realizing that life is not about finding all the answers, and acing the test with a perfect score; it's about procuring one answer, finding it, savoring it, and moving on to the next. Just because more knowledge, more experience, and further understanding opens up new rooms filled with filing cabinets to the ceiling full of even more questions, does not mean we should be discouraged. It should awaken our somnolent souls and remind us how vast and ingenious the universe is. Having more paths to discover shouldn't frighten or weaken us, it should empower and excite us to no end.

# chapter 12

*"In every bit of honest writing in the world, there is a base theme. Try to understand men, if you understand each other you will be kind to each other. Knowing a man well, never leads to hate, and nearly always leads to love."*

~John Steinback

The henchmen of Adolph Hitler were conditioned to hate the Jews and others deemed "lesser" by the state. The whole continent of Europe was gripped by a relentless fist of anti-Semitism. Men all over an entire hemisphere were filled with a hate for a people they had never met, even an historically innocuous and peaceful group of people. The reasons and genesis of this hate are complex and storied, but we know one thing. We know that the idea of love was abandoned, that any attempt to know man was cruelly halted. We also know that in the complete absence of love, poison was inserted into the soil of the earth, germinating into the ultimate sin of mankind: genocide.

So what happens when we decide not to get to know people because we don't agree with their way of life: with their religion, sexual orientation, or other putatively untoward ways of life? It's not like this alone will lead to genocide. Mass murder doesn't come about by one act of bigotry, or by the hands of a few racist individuals. But we should be concerned with more than just the worst case scenario. We should be worried about fostering an environment where hate and mistreatment is permissible. We should be ever concerned about a world where love is becoming less prevalent.

Think about the people you care about the most. Are they not the people you know the best? Sure, sometimes we meet people and are instantly charmed by their charisma and energy, but the people that deep down we would cry for, or take an axe for, are nearly always the people we know the best.

For me these people are my two sisters, my parents, and a handful of friends that I have known for years. Even though they all have their weaknesses and downfalls, they are the type of people that I place on an elevated pedestal, in a glass case far above the ground. They aren't perfect by any means, but they often appear to me to be a flawless group. This is because the time together, memories shared, words exchanged, leave little room for anything besides love.

On the other hand, the people I find most repugnant and annoying are usually people that I have not taken the time to know in any real capacity. And even if I have known them well, I likely have not tried to understand them with any real effort.

Sometimes I find myself in a rather unquiet mood. I'll be walking down a busy sidewalk downtown or typing away on my computer in a restaurant, and for whatever reason the people around me start to bother me. I look at the hipster couple that orders a couple of sodas and I think, "What on earth would compel a woman to shave her head?" Just as this silent thought is finished, I aim and fire at the boyfriend, "When is dyeing your hair blue ever a good idea?" I could have said,

"Hello", asked them where they were from, or even asked the guy where he purchased his snug pair of tan jeans that I actually liked. But I did no such thing. I just waited in line and judged. I didn't hate them, but I certainly didn't love them. The internal dialogue isn't much different as I walk down the city street. I see overweight individuals in ugly footwear and cheap T-shirts. I see businessmen in large groups with sunglasses and what I can only assume is an unattractive smugness. But I don't say hello. I don't ask where they are from, and I don't even smile.

This isn't my usual self. I usually love people, and am curious and open-minded to different cultures and ways of life. But sometimes, if even just for a moment, I am erroneously convinced that the world is really all about me and my problems. I am not concerned with adding happiness to those around me. I am concerned about getting a haircut before the weekend. I don't care about the plight of strangers, I care about paying my rent on time and receiving positive affirmation from a picture I just posted online.

I think the secret to avoiding feelings of hate is in thinking about oneself less. When you think about others, when you try to share joy with others, you will find that you really don't have time or space in your life for negative feelings.

I'm not really worried about genocidal events transpiring in my own life. It's possible, yes, but it certainly isn't an immediate threat or issue in the time and place where I live. But a ubiquitous threat upon all humanity is hate and indifference. Not caring about other people is something that can destroy families, eviscerate confidence, and crush relationships. It doesn't seem that way, because we are usually focused on only what is visible. But life unravels faster than we can imagine in our ever blurred periphery.

There are almost always people suffering at our feet, but we walk past them only looking at the beauty of our own horizon. Even loved ones sometimes tremble and cry without our knowledge because we are too focused on our own existence to ask if they need anything. Friendships go unrealized because we are too proud to introduce ourselves. Relationships never start because we are too scared to compliment someone on how good they look. A whole world is passing us by because we don't care enough about kindness, or because we don't love enough. Most people aren't hateful by nature, but if we do not love with every particle of our being, if we are not seeking out acts of kindness, if we are not getting to know each other, what are we doing? It's like we have the sun in a bottle, but we bury the bottle and reach for a single match.

J.D. Salinger asked a vital question: "Were most of your stars out? Were you busy writing your heart out?" Of course he was referring to the effort of composing a creative piece of art. But I find myself asking the same question for all the efforts in my life. Am I extinguishing all the light I have been given, or is there still brightness in my stars? Am I exhausting my heart in an attempt to make people around me happier? I hope to the God I believe in that I don't end my life without having squeezed out the entirety of the light I have been given. What good is a full vessel that has been cast away?

My stomach curls inward when I think of my days passing away without touching other people's lives. I know no matter how hard I try, there will come a day when I will know I could have done more. I won't be paralyzed by the past, but I want the future to be changed and increased on account of my acts, no matter how small and insignificant they might seem.

In my endless wondering, I think about certain Nazis that survived the war and maybe even evaded punitive actions. I consider the haunting regrets that must circle their thoughts like vultures around a wounded wolf. Many in interviews and writings have held strong to their convictions of military obedience and outright anti-Semitism. Some have revealed painful remorse and regret for their actions that can never be overturned or forgotten. And still many admit to little more than a modicum of moral culpability in interviews bereft of meaningful remorse or believable apology. A member[10] of the Reserve Police Battalion 101[11] rationalized his own actions in a post-war trial statement:

> I made the effort, and it was possible for me, to shoot only children. It so happened that the mothers led the children by the hand. My neighbor then shot the mother and I shot the child that belonged to her, because I reasoned with myself that after all without its mother the child could not live any longer. It was supposed to be, so to speak, soothing to my conscience to release children unable to live without their mothers.

Regardless of ethical viewpoints decades after the fact, there is no doubt that these men and women, many guilty of murder, rape, and assault, are forced to live with what they have done, forced to wonder what their lives would have been like had they acted differently, had they acted out of kindness and not hate, and had they not rationalized the the taking of human lives.

Life moves on hinges buried beneath the ground where sound and reason cannot enter. Things often move and happen so quickly and

---

[10] Known in courtroom documents simply as Friedrich M.

[11] A Nazi German paramilitary group operating under the control of the SS.

without much reason, making life a confusing, yet oddly connected phenomenon. I tend to side with the connectivity of things. For better or worse, I believe in the effect of the butterflies.

*Schindler's List* immortalized the saying, "Whoever saves one life, saves the world entire." This beautiful line of words, however, comes originally from the Talmud and in its entirety reads, "Whoever destroys a soul, it is considered as if he destroyed an entire world. And whoever saves a life, it is considered as if he saved an entire world." Just as we do not know the wonderful ripples that will lie in the lake of life from a righteous or altruistic act, we likewise don't know the pain or suffering that transpires from mistreating someone or neglecting to love someone. It is the butterfly effect in reverse: a theory of wild hypotheticals, a principle of unaccomplished and unrealized consequences.

As the fluttering wings of a tiny creature have been scientifically proven to effect innumerable physical things across the universe, surely daily acts of the most advanced creatures on the planet will have monumental or catastrophic effects on all of humanity for tomorrow and forever.

A seed unplanted can become an unforested land, bereft of beauty and home, without ecosystem and life, left barren and dusty, a worthless patch, all because a seed was not dropped, or because the clouds refused to open.

By that same token, a single undisturbed root can burst up, exploding into a tree, a true paragon of life, a natural obelisk sustaining further life, creating oxygen, making paper that lands on the spines of great books, books that change lives. A tree, a book, a love. All is bloomed. All is possible. All can germinate from a single act, and all can occur from an act undone or a word unspoken.

This is life. Much is beyond our capacity to touch. And very much of what we do touch will go unseen or unnoticed. But a magnificent amount of what we do will cause a stir in the world we know. Whether it is a fine and delightful stir, or a malignant and awful stir, is up to us.

I am often subtly impressed and inspired by small acts in the distance, by overheard declarations, and adjacent kindness. I view all people and things as this sort of beautiful raw and unfiltered material for writing, so I observe a lot. I try to notice how people interact, and how strangers connect with other strangers. While looking at the world through this authorial kaleidoscope, I come to realize how much people see and hear us without us ever knowing. We aren't unlike some rare blue bird with a brightly colored beak flying in with mysterious beauty, and flying away almost instantly. We might be alone in a café reading all day. And though we are alone and quiet, we are being noticed by dozens of unique people. Most may not notice anything besides the space we take up or the fact that we are wearing an attractive scarf or a clean pair of shoes. But others will notice things. They will see the joy we receive in turning a simple page; they might notice a smile come across our face as a thoughtful text appears on our phone. Perhaps they will overhear a brief conversation we have on the phone between chapters, a moment where we are sheltered in the vulnerability of expressing love to a parent, a parent that aches when we aren't anything but happy. Maybe what we do all day in relative solitude at a coffee shop will have little consequence over the lives of others. But maybe someone will remember that book they need to read, maybe someone will be touched by a few words whispered to a loved one. Maybe a small smile on our faces will be enough to shed light on the shadows of someone's dark day.

All of this sounds kind of romantic and unlikely. But let's consider more realistic scenarios, more interactive moments. Many of us often feel overlooked, under-appreciated and frustratingly unnoticed at times. Maybe our family lives in Michigan and our friends aren't being good friends. Alas, day after day we go to work or school or the pharmacy and people see us and notice us. So whether we are feeling particularly important or not, we should remember that our acts could still inspire many. Those many may never leave us a thank you note or publicly sing our praises, but good is good even if it is not formally recognized.

So in all things we do, hopefully we can remember that there is often an audience. We can say, "Who cares, I'm gonna do me," or we can try to better the world that we occupy. Our lives are made up of the tens of thousands of tiny moments that seem inconsequential, that seem to have no bearing on the progression of mankind, but these moments of kindness, of unbridled laughter, of unnecessary generosity, these are the main pieces of our life's puzzle. This is how you change the world. So be mindful, and try to live an existence that could inspire a downtrodden onlooker, a person you may never see again in this mortal sphere. And just like the footprint of Neil Armstrong that remains untouched and intact on the floor of the moon, we too can leave an indelible footprint on our own planet.

# chapter 13

*"A bridge of silver wings stretches from the dead ashes of an unforgiving nightmare to the jeweled vision of a life started anew."*

~Aberjhani

One of my favorite parts about reading and studying the Holocaust is in discovering and learning about life after tragedy. Decades after the fact, thousands and thousands of souls who saw the crimson swastikas in person, and smelled the vile breath of angry Nazis, deal with their personal tragedy. In far-reaching corners of the earth widows still grieve, mothers write down their daily sorrow, and grown children lecture and teach about what they saw and lived through. The lives of victims are as unique and varied as any group of people that have existed. Some have lost their once immutable faith, some have stayed in their native countries, others have immigrated to far off lands. Some have done terrible things in the wake of their trials, while others have moved mountains in the name of goodness.

No one knows the true scope of suffering endured by those who saw the alabaster teeth of the Holocaust and lived. The miracles are not just in the stories of survivors, but in the basic fact that they survived. Whether they share their story with no one, or publish memoirs and essays, the world is different and better for it.

I suppose the crux of my intrigue is in seeing someone, anyone, begin again. I love the poetic justice of thriving after all was lost, the notion of defeating demons of yesteryear, the victory in simply trying again, in having the courage to start over, is eternally admirable.

We've all been there. We have all been forced to start over in some capacity. We have all faced the ghastly reality of having to begin once again. And as a writer, I am back to thinking about myself. I sit here and think about when I have had to truly start over. And this is perhaps where it is most applicable, because most people are not heroes, and most people have led, at least at first sight, unremarkable lives, with basic stories of winning and losing, of crying and rejoicing.

Back to me. When I was fourteen, my family quite suddenly moved from Phoenix to the tiny rural town of Monroe, Utah. I thought my life was certainly over. All my stuff was in storage until my Dad sold our house, and I was a skinny fourteen year old barely above five feet starting high school without a single friend. I was starting over. I was nervous and lost. My first day of school I donned a backpack while the rest of the student body carried their books to and from their lockers. I ate lunch by myself, not knowing whether I should align myself with the Native American kids that were known colloquially as "dorm students," or one of the other lunchtime groups that seemed desperate for attention. I vied to sit alone, but at the same table as ten or fifteen cool looking kids. I thought someone might come over and recognize that I was a fish from different waters. But people just looked. I had moved a lot growing up, but this seemed worse than any scary first day of school I had ever had.

The food was cold and terrible and there was no sign of encroaching friendship, so I decided to abort my plan and get something out of the vending machine and maybe cruise the halls, avoiding the appearance of loneliness and timidity. I made a loop around the tiny high school and found the vending machine. I pressed C5 in hopes that Cheez-Its would at least make me feel a little better about my day. I don't know if I misspressed or if the cruel machine malfunctioned, but from the top shelf fell the worst item in the whole machine, Boston Baked Beans. At a loss, I grabbed my worthless snack, perched myself against a red locker and popped some candies in my mouth. Kids walked past me and I tried as hard as I could not to cry. Starting over sucked. As the days grew into weeks that I thought would never accumulate to years, the boys who openly disliked me started to accept me into their tribe. An easiness towards humor and the game of basketball changed high school for me. I knew I wouldn't be a pariah forever. But when you are fourteen, one afternoon in the halls, one moment in the locker room, one rejection at the school dance can feel like a sweltering eternity. But beginning anew, forced into freshness and awkward corners, helped me grow. Life is starting over all the time. We don't always realize it, but we have to start over a million times in a lifetime; it's just that some starts sting and scar us more than others. An end or an unwanted beginning can crack and break us, but it is those difficult endings and unbearable starts that leave us better men and women, it's those that shape our lives like the sculptor's pick.

I recently went for a walk late at night to clear my head of its more noxious weeds and to work out some unsatisfactory paragraphs in my mind. Not thirty seconds into my night wander I looked up at the magnificently full moon. I thought of how this giant celestial orb symbolized change, starting over, and beginning again. I quickly grabbed my phone and opened up my notes section as to not lose the inspiration that had trickled down from the skies, almost waiting for me to take a walk at 1:20 a.m. In a writer's rush I jotted down the following thought:

> The ancient moon is a wondrous reminder of the fact that it's okay to start over. A moon wanes and falters with the passing days, almost shying away from the unknown of the night, at least to part of the woken earth. But as the lunar cycle continues and presses on, the moon returns from its crescent recesses and shines again. It starts over. It's cyclical for her, the mighty Luna. So it is with man. The only difference is that our cycles are not as predictable and sure. But just as the moon shall return in full spherical splendor, we too can start our lives over, and bare our faces again.

The same lessons I learned through the painful pubescent years preceding college, I learned staring at the clear purple black sky. People learn in so many ways, but all around us are stark reminders and lessons. We just have to be interested in picking up the signals. I myself prefer not to wait for lessons to smack me in the jaw, though they certainly will from time to time. I would rather seek them out in great books and awesome speeches, museums and walks through Berlin at night. I have been ranting and professing on how much you can learn from specific events of tragedy and sorrow, but the important thing is that you learn, that you seek and that you set your mind on fire. And if a sad defeated woman in her nineties retelling her story about moving to America penniless after surviving the horrors of multiple concentration camps can help you realize your life isn't so hard, or help you understand how starting over can be treacherous, but worthwhile, then listen. Then read. Then learn.

Starting over comes in many different sizes, varying fonts, and contrasting colors. I have had breakups that I thought I would not easily be put back together from, relationships that left me void of hope and curiously disenchanted with the things around me. Investing emotionality with another human being, becoming best friends, only to find yourself rather unallowed to talk to that very person, that is a hell of its own. Suddenly you are cut off and it hurts, and the thought of starting from square one with someone who will never smell like the one you lost, who will never smile at you with the precise folding of dimples and settling of slightly crooked teeth like the one who walked away, kills you. But what choice do you have? You have to start over. Or decide that your life is meaningless and surcease all movement towards a somewhat happy life. But that's no way to live, and you know it.

    I've moved from city to city all over the map, starting over in new towns, new universities, new churches, and new apartment complexes. And each time it kind of sucks, it kind of kills a small part of you to move onto a new chapter when you aren't necessarily ready, and when you aren't so sure the plot necessitates a new chapter to move forward. But the author of your life isn't concerned with the rosiness and fluidity of your story. He is concerned with the endgame, the lessons learned in the journey, not the specific chronology and smoothness of things. So with this understanding, or at least partial cognizance, I have started over again and again. I have started over a thousand times each year, it seems, and then a few more unexpected times. But this is life, and expecting anything else is a daffy way to think. The problem is we live and operate in unconscious patterns, and we can get used to a life without much shift, without any going against the grain as it were. Changes and forced beginnings are terrifying and blunt. But there is no other way for life to be. Without wind or the tides, the earth could not function properly, and would soon fall to waste and terrestrial decomposition. The same goes for the winds of change and tides of opportunity in our own lives: without them we would lead meaningless lives. Our minds would atrophy, and our spirits would wither and surrender to the vices of everyday life. Our sheer boredom would sink us into a pit of monotony. Our health would deteriorate and every dream we ever had would evaporate in the night. Without change, without toil and trial, life would not be.

As I walked through the muggy barracks of Auschwitz, I thought about individuals. I thought about the lucky ones, those who survived the contrived evil of the Nazi machine. I say lucky, but many who survived considered themselves the unlucky ones, witnesses to the murder of their own families, and helpless victims of an indelible past. I looked up and down the barracks, the wood and concrete, and the coldness of the space pricked me in spite of the summertime heat. I stood alone in a crowd of people and wondered what life after the war would have been like for the survivors. Many remained unwanted in their hometowns with little or no resources to start over. But I knew they did it anyway. They moved on, many to Israel or America, and some sadly rusticated to their ruinous European towns of origin, towns forgotten, diseased and scattered. Though their minds and bodies were stripped of everything, they would live on. They would persevere and forever be victors over their many enemies and circumstances.

The tears that wanted to cascade down my face in that awful camp swelled up in my eye sockets because I knew I had changes to make, and new beginnings to endure, and not a one could compare with those men and women whose invisible footsteps I retraced that day in Auschwitz —a place supposedly named centuries earlier after a Slavic man who owned a large wooden fortress known in medieval times as a gord[12]. I wondered how terrible this long forgotten person would feel knowing his family name had been corrupted, Germanized and turned into a byword for horror and manslaughter. Of course he would have no way of knowing, no way of foreseeing this grim conclusion. Nevertheless, I imagine this medieval man with dark hair, Slavic facial features, and tough skin learning of his name's tragic future in a saddening dream, some subconscious yet knowing spirit from beyond revealing to him the unimaginable fate. And though he is guiltless, he falls to the ground and weeps uncontrollably. Prostrated and confused, he cries not for his own damnation, but for the fate of the world. As he returns to his bedside he predicts that one day they will refer to that future era as the dark ages.

---

[12] A medieval Slavonic fortress usually made of wood.

# chapter 14

*"But this is true too: Stories can save us."*

~John H. Arnold

As Nazism started to spread through Europe and the laws and dogma of Hitler came to the forefront, innocent Jews and other "undesirables," such as Poles, Slavs, Jehovah's Witnesses, criminals, dissidents, and gypsies, were all getting arrested and violently corralled into camps, ad hoc brothels, crammed ghettos, and myriad institutions of imprisonment. A portion of the world was being torn asunder by the gross hands of avarice and hate while the rest of the earth ignored the blood pouring down the streets or slept undisturbed and unaware.

Meanwhile in thousands of villages, cities, and hamlets throughout the European continent, the Gestapo reigned supreme. They, being the extension of Hitler that would execute round-ups, make arrests, and compile files on the persons in question, were the people to be feared: the men and women that could sign one's death warrant, or set one free by the whimsy of a pen, or the steel of handcuffs, or threat of a bullet. There was no limit to the reasons the Gestapo could legally stop someone on the street, or deem persons guilty of crimes against the state. What often and ultimately determined the fate of many imprisoned persons was whether their file on record contained two onerous words: *rückkehr unerwünscht* or simply '*RU*' meaning return not desired.

Though these words didn't guarantee an execution, they were a calloused way of reminding the Nazi desk jockeys that the human in question was essentially disposable, not useful for their present needs and rather a burden and scourge that would just as well be eradicated whenever convenience permitted.

Most camp prisoners, ghetto dwellers, and otherwise detained individuals would never have the opportunity to see their files and read those ugly words; in fact, many did not know German and wouldn't know the difference if they did get their cold and brittle hands on those life-determining documents.

These euphemistic words summoning innocent people to their final breaths were a typical example of how the Nazi regime valued human life. If people didn't somehow help the German cause, no matter how distorted and sinuous that cause was, they were discarded and stamped like an old out of date textbook that no library cared for anymore. The Nazis were also masters of linguistic manipulation. They wanted everyone to think that Jews and other assumed political enemies were not wanted by anyone, and that their return to whatever homeland they possessed was entirely unnecessary and undesired by anyone. But who were they speaking for? Who can say with some master voice that someone's safe return home is not desired, besides those people waiting for them in their homes with outstretched limbs and tears of happiness? Who can do that? Well, when evil spreads, reason and rites fall by the eroded wayside and humanity is forced to either fight back or accept it as new doctrine.

We all are guilty of allowing evil into our lives without fighting, without waving our arms in an effort to halt its progression. Instead we sit back and slowly let the new way, the evil way, indoctrinate us. Sometimes the evils are large, and sometimes they are so small they seem innocuous and trite. But at our worst we are not totally unlike the guilty men of so many yesterdays.

This notion of one's return not being desired resonated with me when I first read it. I had never heard such simple yet painful phraseology in all my readings of Adolf Hitler and the Third Reich. It made me think past the horridness of the Holocaust and the war and into my own life. Though it is infinitely less relevant to the world, my own life is always much more on the mind and much more relatable. I thought about relationships. I thought about times when I wanted to return to someone or something, but the simple truth was that I wasn't wanted, my return was not desired. It hurt me to recall certain things. But I did anyway.

My mind was already caught up in its own confusing form of pity and reflection, a state that feels both cathartic and painful at the same time, like listening to a song you love that reminds you of a very specific and raw heartbreak. I thought about a girl that I had treated poorly. I liked her for months and probably could have loved her if I would have just let myself. But I convinced myself that she was not the one for me and broke her heart, not once, but twice. I cared about her more than anyone, but I watched her walk away. She kissed me on the mouth and said, "Tell me to stay," with her hands on the wheel of an idling car, the backseat full of her every last belonging, and I couldn't muster a single coherent word. She looked at me with knowing eyes. She knew it was over. I knew it was over. And she drove away. She drove home, and almost immediately fell in love with a redheaded kid with nicer abs than me. I just wanted her to be happy, but seeing her happy with *him* did anything but make me happy. I moved on, I really did. But still, a large part of me wanted her back. I even made some juvenile attempts to reach out to her. But she made it clear that I blew it and my return to her was not desired. Though it was fair and deserving, that feeling still stung in a most lingering way. Everybody wants to be wanted. Even when it isn't right, you would like to think that you were the very sine quo non of that person's life, an irreplaceable pearl that would be welcomed back the very second one made it known that a return was desired. But that isn't reality; in fact, it's almost always an absurd fantasy that we know is absurd, but we believe it anyway to make ourselves feel better.

    Being unwanted and undesired can be one of the most painful things a person ever goes through, akin to disembowelment and broken femurs. In life we expect tragic patterns. We know that people around us will die. We know that we too will one day pass away. And we know that sadness and tragedy is all around us, and sickeningly omnipresent. And though at a certain stage in life we start to understand that rejection and indifference are a real part of life, it still seems like we are being blindsided whenever someone or something truly makes us feel unwanted and emotionally aborted. That's why every breakup hurts in its own mind-chillingly unique way. That's why a disowned child can't get past the fact that his parents, those humans who once loved and cherished this tiny human, now want nothing to do with him. It's a pernicious little nuance of the human experience: the mere fact that loneliness, human connection, acceptance, love, are all so vital to our state of felicity. Why can't we just be roaming emotionless vagabonds that don't need anyone? Why can't society function without the need to make people feel like they are a part of something? Maybe a life like that sounds ideal for a minute, but that would be no life worth living. We aren't isolated rocks in the middle of a barren field, objects that thrive off of nothing and contribute to nothing, we are fully developed humans that can do more than any organism or contrived entity has ever done or ever will do on this or any other planet. So it is imperative to take that knowledge and move forward. If feeling unwanted, jilted, and discarded is such a loathsome thing to us, why would we carelessly inflict that anguish on others?

Certainly it's easier said than done. But how extraordinary would our existence be if every place we stepped foot in wanted us there, and wanted us to come back again and again. Of course it's not totally reasonable to imagine a world like this. But a portion, a tiny fraction of any fantastic and unrealistic dream can manifest itself with great effort. And isn't a fraction of paradise better than worlds of hell? Maybe you feel like you cannot change the world with pretty ideas and utopian pipe dreams. But you can change your household. You can alter your world, which by the laws of nature will change things around it, spreading whatever microscopic portion of the utopian pie you are promoting.

I think of my late Grandmother Darlene, a woman that seemed to make everything better with very little effort, a woman that loved unconditionally every person she came across. Her passing was sudden and heart-breaking. And being around my grieving grandfather, a small man with a full head of white hair and a proud scar on his jawline, I could feel how much she was missed. I could feel the sadness and I imagined how much everyone must have wished she could come back. What a wonderful legacy to leave, just the fact that her absence was so painful testified as to the type of person she was. It made me wonder how I could get to that elevated place, a far off place where all I left in my wake was love and good memories.

Again those words linger in my mind, suspended on a floating piece of beige paper in tiny faded ink, *return not desired*. No soul on earth could say that about my Grandma. But what if she had grown up Jewish, in a small town in Romania or Poland, while a certain demagogue ran an entire continent? What if her father, my great grandfather, Christian though he was, was part of some resistance group making young Darlene another disposable piece of labor according to the Nazi code of hate? It seems so impossible to envision any alternate history where my sweet Grandma wasn't loved and admired by all. How could she ever be hated and abused? It made no sense. Yet how many grandmothers, innocent teenagers just discovering love, or sick tired old men were part of the "undesirables", people deemed as useless and irrelevant as rodents?

My heart quivered and cried thinking of this impossible revisionist version of history. I had seen pictures of my father's mother as a child. She was freckled, pale and extremely skinny. As a teenager she was an undiscovered silent movie star, living her 1940's reality on a dusty farm raising sheep and cultivating beets in South Central Utah. Was her life that different than a Hilde or Sofia born at the same time, but an ocean away? Biased though I am, I know wonderful women, boys and girls of all forms exist all over the world, the type of people that you want to meet, but so rarely do, the type of people that are confusingly selfless in the most unflashy and unexpected of ways. And the fact that so many of these choice humans were set aside for tragedy, forgotten and unwanted by mere chance of birth, by the sheer whimsy of location, kills me. I don't empathize because I too am Jewish, or because I've been crudely persecuted, but because I too have a mother. I too have people whose death and torture would elicit the most awful erumpent of cries and deep squeals. I too have lost a loved one, and I too have loved in the most proper way. As different as every human is, and as misunderstood as many of us feel, we are all the same, just different shapes. Do not all trees stretch upwards toward the vast ethers, secreting oxygen, casting shadows, and catching water from the clouds? But do they concern themselves with distant forests that aren't as lush, or with the tree to their left whose branches have fallen? They do not, for they are all trees. They all create new things, and they all live until they die.

# chapter 15

*"People think dreams aren't real just because they aren't made of matter, of particles. Dreams are real. But they are made of viewpoints, of images, of memories and puns and lost hopes."*

~Neil Gaiman

Dreams have a strange way of portending things. You don't have to be a prophet or mystical soothsayer to receive telling dreams or visions of your own future. Dreams are but regurgitations of our own thoughts and sundry movements in life. Though it is true that most of our nocturnal thoughts and subconscious ponderings will either be forgotten, seemingly erased by the zing of our alarm clock, or discarded as a sort of muddled and useless mental pulp.

Oh, but sometimes a dream is too vivid to forget upon awakening, too odd to ignore, or too potent to not wake you in the darkest part of the night, covering your blanketed body in sweat, causing fear or sudden tears. Dreams can be the angels we need or the demons we loathe, or they can just be the cats we see every day on our way to work, a swirling disconnect of minutia.

More than 500 days after I sat down in Poland and wrote about a dream that moved me, I sit up late and type out the final words of a book that germinated from a single dream. And maybe the dream wasn't as poetic and deeply meaningful as I thought it was, but if nothing else it gave me a reason and a place to start with this book. So I sit and reflect one more time on that eerie dream I had the night before I walked into Auschwitz. The fear I felt, the helplessness, the chaos, it is all as clear to me today as the meal I had yesterday. And the allegory is clear to me. I had spent so many hours learning about Holocaust survivors and their lives, reading about their personal hells, their endless chaos and their shattered existences, but I'd never really lived or experienced it past the page.

My dream that woke me up in a feverish moment of fright in a cramped hotel room in east-central Poland prepared me and reminded me that though I would come even closer to understanding the great plight of the Hebrew people, it would be but a tiny drop in the ocean.

But still, I was thankful for my dream and my experiences. I recalled something Mother Teresa had said about our efforts being so small and irrelevant: "What we do is nothing but a drop in the ocean. But if we didn't do it, the ocean would be one drop less than it is."

People say that their summer abroad in Paris changed their lives, or that volunteering at an orphanage in Zimbabwe made them a different person. And though that sounds fairly reasonable, those of us who have travelled little and served even less silently scoff at their unrealistic changes of heart and over-exaggerated personal discoveries and pseudo epiphanies.

But what a godawful way to look at people and the universe. If a weekend in Mexico City changed your best friend's point of view, how wonderful, how great. Are people not capable of change? Who cares what spurs that change. I believe the smallest things this world delivers to us can change us forever if we but decide to let them. I've been changed by a book, a mere sentence of pure truth, a timely song. I was recently changed a little by seeing a thirty-five year old man hug his mother, both with eyes red and wet, grieving a loved one. That tiny witnessed moment altered my life in some meaningful, albeit small way.

I have a friend who told me about a single sunset that changed him. In tears I heard him say he knew that God painted that for him in a dark hour of his life.

If the tiniest things can change us, how dare we mitigate the truly big things in other people's journeys. As surely as a chance encounter has changed my own life, a walk through the gas chambers in Auschwitz undoubtedly has changed me indelibly and forever, making me a better person than I was before.

People talk a lot about defining moments, these hard to describe instances where things shift in cosmically large ways, but truthfully, every waking moment of our lives are defining moments. Our job is to recognize the bigger moments, bask in the beautiful moments and be ready for the turning points, the ones that can if we only let them, change us forever.

Auschwitz did that for me. It was more than a moment, more than a special day, it was a punch you in the soul, spit on your past renaissance, that changed me forever.

**the end**

Made in the USA
San Bernardino, CA
05 October 2016